Toby Meadows is a Director of Three's Company (Creative Consultants) Ltd, providing consultancy services to the fashion industry, and a Director of the womenswear label Belle & Bunty. He is also an Associate Lecturer at the London College of Fashion, where he writes and delivers short courses for professional development within the fashion industry.

Published in 2009 by
Laurence King Publishing Ltd
361–373 City Road
London EC1V 1LR
United Kingdom
Tel: + 44 20 7841 6900
Fax: + 44 20 7841 6910
e-mail: enquiries@laurenceking.com
www.laurenceking.com

A catalogue record for this book is available
from the British Library

ISBN-13: 978-1-85669-575-6

Designed by TwoSheds Design

Printed in China

HOW TO SET UP & RUN A

FASHION LABEL

Toby Meadows

Laurence King Publishing

Contents

*Ed Hardy catwalk show
at trade show Bread & Butter*

Introduction: Find Your Way

Running a successful fashion label requires around 90 per cent business acumen and only about 10 per cent artistic ability. Most fashion start-ups are managed by the designers themselves who, whilst strong on the design front, may have only a very rudimentary understanding of the business of fashion, especially in the all-important formative years. As a result, although thousands of talented fashion designers and technicians graduate every year, most new fashion start-ups fail.

The aim of this book is to bridge the gap between the design and business sides of running your own label. It offers a realistic overview of the key elements needing research, development and nurturing in the context of your own business to give your fashion label a chance to compete favourably within a demanding, unforgiving and competitive industry. It should act as a guide through those initial tricky years and help you create a strong foundation from which your fashion label can flourish.

By working through the book, reading the case studies and undertaking the tasks, you will gain an understanding of what your next steps should be and what challenges lie on the road ahead. This book will give you the tools to focus your ideas and ultimately help you find the right way to grow and develop your fashion business.

Shuttershades

Chapter 1: Introduction to the Fashion Industry

*U*nderstanding the fashion industry and exactly where your new label will sit is fundamental to getting your product and business right. You will need to take your time and do the research (see Chapter 7) to understand where the potential for your product will be and how buyers, journalists and consumers will expect it to be presented to them. This chapter will introduce you to three of the key market segments: haute couture, ready-to-wear and mass market, and will touch on the growing interest in eco fashion. It will look at the areas of fashion design and seasonality before moving on to the importance of the supply chain.

Market Segments

From the very beginning you will need to decide at which level to position your label. Many of your subsequent management decisions will be dictated by consumer expectation and will shape your business strategy. The three main market segments are haute couture, ready-to-wear and mass market, with significant numbers of sub-levels in the latter two markets, offering a great deal of variation in product and pricing.

Haute Couture

The term 'haute couture' describes luxurious, elaborately detailed and finished one-off pieces, combined with sometimes extravagant designs. Born out of the first fashion houses to set up in Paris in the late nineteenth century, couture is still at the very upper end of the fashion spectrum, servicing the very few who can afford the luxurious creations that are fitted specifically to the client's every measurement. More importantly, however, for those few remaining members of the couture family, the haute couture shows in Paris represent an opportunity to showcase their design talent and act as a reminder of the immense creative ability of the designers behind the labels.

In France haute couture is a protected term, which can be officially used only by designers who meet well-defined standards set by the Chambre Syndicale de la Couture. The terms 'bespoke' and 'made-to-measure' may also be used for any garment that is created for a specific client, but are quite often found in the realms of menswear. To add to the confusion, many designers say their work is haute couture when, technically, it is not, and made-to-measure can also describe a service whereby ready-to-wear garments are adjusted to fit the specific needs of the customer.

Belle & Bunty on the catwalk

Ready-To-Wear

Ready-to-wear, otherwise known as prêt-à-porter, became a viable alternative to haute couture in the 1960s when fashion houses started to showcase designs that came in a range of standard sizes that could be bought directly from boutiques. By doing away with the necessity of long fitting sessions, ready-to-wear was far less expensive and therefore instantly more accessible to a wider audience. Most of the designer fashion bought today is considered ready-to-wear. Whereas couture is still shown twice a year in Paris, ready-to-wear is showcased all around the world at a number of different fashion weeks, principally in New York, London, Paris and Milan. Today, ready-to-wear is a cross between haute couture and the mass market. Although not made for the individual, great care and detail is taken in the design and finishing, and the numbers of each garment produced tend to be low, thereby making them exclusive and expensive.

The larger, high-end designer ready-to-wear labels also develop diffusion ranges to sell at a low to mid price point. Examples of this are Marc by Marc Jacobs and See by Chloé. By creating a separate label, designers are able to tap into a much larger consumer base while protecting the aspirational brand identity they have created for their main line.

Ready-to-wear labels often wholesale their collections to boutiques and department stores by showcasing at the fashion weeks held seasonally twice a year. Typically they work 12 months in advance, researching and developing their collection for the trade fairs at which they will sell, then going into production when they have taken forward orders from the boutiques and department stores. This allows them to produce only the number of garments ordered, thereby minimising the risk of overproduction as well as the initial expense in outlay to their manufacturer. Many designers also open their own retail outlets, allowing them to give their complete offer directly to the consumer and maximising their margins by cutting out the middleman.

Show Calendar (Northern Hemisphere)

Month	Show	Season
January	Couture (Paris)	Spring/summer
February/March	Ready-to-wear — all	Autumn/winter
July	Couture (Paris)	Autumn/winter
September/October	Ready-to-wear — all	Spring/summer

Examples of internationally renowned ready-to-wear labels include Chloé, Gucci, Ralph Lauren and Burberry. However, ready-to-wear is now an extremely diverse market with a number of sub-levels, including luxury, high-end, mid-level and premium design. Each level will distinguish brands by product offer, price points, marketing strategies and distribution outlets.

High-street retailers like
Burton adapt trends taken
from high-end designers and
mass produce them

Mass Market

Today most people wear mass market fashion, which caters for an even wider range of customers than ready-to-wear. Clothes are produced in very large quantities and in a good range of standard sizing, making them less expensive and more accessible to the average consumer. Designers often adapt the trends set by the big names in fashion at the high end of the market. By being creative with cheaper materials and production techniques, and by working hard to stay within their customers' taste levels, they are able to produce affordable fashion. However, mass market designers cannot rely solely on inspiration from the leading catwalk designers, and are always looking at other areas for trend inspiration.

Mass market fashion is produced first and then sold through retail distribution outlets, typically owned by the brand (Topshop, H&M, Zara, Gap, and so on). A large element of risk is involved, as it is difficult to predict exactly what product will be sold. However, by designing, manufacturing and then selling the product at retail prices, the brand will make the biggest profit margins available whilst offering flexibility in pricing to maintain competitiveness.

Your product line will fit somewhere within these three broad markets. Working out which market and researching it thoroughly is your starting point. Your research will identify a number of smaller sub-markets and even niche markets within each. One such market, developing rapidly and breaking into bigger mainstream markets, is eco fashion.

Eco Fashion

'Eco fashion' refers to fashionable and stylish clothing manufactured using environmentally-friendly processes under free trade conditions and is becoming a growing force in the market. At its extreme it can mean recycled clothing and even recycled materials, such as eco-fleeces produced from recycled plastic bottles. It has recently taken on greater importance, with a number of designers looking to work with environmentally-friendly materials and processes. As consumers become more aware of the processes involved in making clothes and the potential carbon footprint of manufacturing overseas, eco fashion is becoming more commonplace and is in itself a marketing tool to attract customers, whether they are interested in high-end or mass market design. Organisations such as the Ethical Fashion Forum (EFF) enable designers, businesses and organisations to focus on social and environmental sustainability in the fashion industry.

The emergence of exhibitions like estethica at London Fashion Week shows the growing importance of the eco and ethical fashion movement

Product Areas of Fashion Design

Whilst the fashion industry offers a broad spectrum of product categories from which you can choose to start your business, you would be wise to start by focusing on just one area. The more specific the market you target, the greater the chance of developing a strong message for your label and delivering a great product to your buyers, press and consumers alike.

Different product categories may also have different selling seasons – which means different buyers and press to attract and more manufacturers to oversee, all of which takes a great deal of time, energy and money to do well. Once your label has established a strong base you may well then look to increase your product range, but consider areas that will complement your existing offer. If you are selling women's eveningwear, complementary products may include shoes, bags, jewellery and perfume. The chart below shows the typical areas that many new fashion start-ups choose to specialise in.

Product Areas for Fashion Design

Area	Brief	Market
Women's daywear	Practical, comfortable, fashionable	Haute couture, ready-to-wear, mass market
Women's eveningwear	Glamorous, sophisticated, right for the occasion	Haute couture, ready-to-wear, mass market
Women's lingerie	Glamorous, comfortable, washable	Haute couture, ready-to-wear, mass market
Men's daywear	Casual, practical, comfortable	Tailoring, ready-to-wear, mass market
Men's eveningwear	Smart, elegant, formal, right for the occasion	Tailoring, ready-to-wear, mass market
Boys' wear	Practical, hard-wearing, washable, inexpensive	Ready-to-wear, mass market
Girls' wear	Pretty, colourful, practical, washable, inexpensive	Ready-to-wear, mass market
Teenage wear	Highly fashion-conscious, comfortable, inexpensive	Ready-to-wear, mass market
Sportswear	Comfortable, practical, well-ventilated, washable	Ready-to-wear, mass market
Knitwear	Right weight and colour for the season	Ready-to-wear, mass market
Outerwear	Stylish, warm, right weight and colour for the season	Ready-to-wear, mass market
Bridalwear	Sumptuous, glamorous, classic	Haute couture, ready-to-wear, mass market
Accessories	Striking, fashionable	Haute couture, ready-to-wear, mass market

Source: *The Fashion Handbook*

Fashion labels Schumacher and Karen Walker (see pages 90 and 136) started off with just a few key pieces and have grown very cleverly from there. Buyers and consumers will always look for quality over quantity, so focus and refine your offer as much as possible when first starting out.

Designer Karen Walker, despite starting off with clothing alone, has branched into sunglasses and jewellery amongst other products

Seasonality

Traditionally a fashion season is defined by weather patterns, with designers typically working to two seasons a year – autumn/winter and spring/summer. By separating these seasons, the key fabrics, colours and shapes can be determined by geographical weather patterns. It is quite typical for established designers to introduce a high summer range as well as a festive season collection, increasing the number of seasons to four.

In retail management, however, a season may be looked at more from a financial perspective. A retail manager will identify a season in terms of a period of time during which the product is sold at full price, at a reduced price, and at clearance price. Determining a product's shelf-life is important. If demand continues, stock will need to be replenished, while stock that is not selling will have to be promoted to clear.

Typical Designer Trading Year (Northern Hemisphere)

Season	Calendar
Autumn/winter	August to January
Festive range (optional)	November
Spring/summer	January to July
High summer (optional)	May/June

Typical Fast Fashion Trading Year (Northern Hemisphere)

Season	Calendar
Early spring	January/February
Spring	February/March
Early summer	April/May
Summer sale	June
High summer	July
Transitional autumn	July/August
Autumn	September/October
Party wear	November
Christmas/transitional spring	December
Winter sale	December/January

The mid 1990s saw a revolution in the way major high-street retailers deliver fashion seasons to the consumer. The 'fast fashion' movement has meant a move away from the traditional two seasons a year in favour of shorter seasons taking place more frequently. Fast fashion allows major retailers, such as H&M, Zara and Topshop, to offer new ranges every few weeks. It also allows them to

1.BUSINESS STRATEGY

2.MARKET RESEARCH

3.DESIGN DEVELOPMENT

follow trends more closely by adapting very quickly to market changes and, more importantly, to control their stock levels more efficiently.

It is still too early to determine exactly how the fast fashion movement will affect the higher end of the fashion market but it has certainly changed how many consumers are buying their fashion. Many designers and high-end retailers have begun to place a great deal of importance on pre-collections, introducing products a couple of months before the major catwalk shows take place (see Chapter 11). Fast fashion has also raised the expectation of value for money, as many high-street retailers are able to offer trend-driven product at very cheap prices with an ever-improving standard of quality.

The key to success in delivering to these new fast fashion seasonal timelines is your supply chain. The better and faster your supply chain, the more flexibility your business will have and the greater the opportunity to offer more collections in a year. Even if, like most small labels, you will be working to a two-season-a-year sales strategy, your supply chain will be of the highest importance to your success.

The Supply Chain

'Supply chain' is the term used to describe the process of planning, implementing and controlling the flow and storage of your products, from their point of origin to their point of consumption, in order to meet your customers' needs. It has taken on more importance with the current trend for offshore production and fast fashion, and is very closely monitored by big high-street retailers. You must manage your supply chain effectively if you are to maximise profit margins and minimise wastage. Supply chains can seem very complicated, but the illustration on these pages shows a basic supply chain for a small fashion start-up that is wholesaling its product twice a year to boutiques, independent retailers and department stores.

The process starts with defining your business strategy – what it is you aim to do. This will be your fashion label's raison d'être, and every other activity you undertake should always be carried out with this in mind. From here you will research your market, including customers and product, to help develop your collections. Only when you have done the research should you move on to the design development stage, when the aesthetics of your range will start to become apparent. The sampling stage often runs alongside the design

4.SAMPLING

development stage for many labels, when your two-dimensional designs will be turned into three-dimensional prototypes. Once these have been developed, the wholesale selling season can begin. Orders will be taken and your collection will need to go into production ready for delivery to the stores. Whilst your production is underway, your PR and marketing for the season's collection should begin in earnest to ensure you are achieving the press you need to entice customers. Once the product lands in-store the retail sales period starts, giving the consumer access to your product and, you hope, leading to high sales and profits for the retailers. Good sales of your product will lead to reorders for next season.

As you move through the chapters of this book, each stage of the supply chain should become more apparent and the key elements for each stage will be explained in greater depth.

5.WHOLESALE SEASON SELLING

6.PRODUCTION

8.PR & MARKETING

7.DISTRIBUTION

The supply chain will play a massive part in your fashion business and your management of it will go a long way towards determining the success of your label

9.RETAIL SELLING SEASON

Case Study: Noir

Peter Ingwersen set up Noir Illuminati II in February 2005 at the age of 41. Having studied design in his native Denmark, Peter did stints as Brand Manager for Levi's before becoming Managing Director at renowned Danish brand Day Birger et Mikkelsen. He left the relative safety of developing others' brands to follow his dream of launching 'a sophisticated, edgy and ethical luxury brand for women aged 30-plus and at a luxury entry price, targeting international leading department stores and boutiques.' Within his first season Noir would be represented in Harvey Nichols (London), Lane Crawford (Hong Kong), Podium (Moscow) and 30 other prestigious retailers around the world. After three years, the number of stores stocking Noir has almost doubled and Peter is discussing proposals for his first retail outlet.

Peter's vision for his label stems from his desire 'to show the world that ethics and style can go hand in hand' and 'to be the first brand to turn corporate social responsibility sexy'. He recognised that there was beginning to be a change in consumers' behaviour, resulting in a demand for more meaningful fashion, 'where the rules of the fashion industry were obeyed but with a social responsibility across the full supply chain'. He set out to create what he felt the fashion industry was missing, a collection that bridged the gap between 'style and ethics', and the result was a merger of two concepts: Noir, Peter's vision for a luxury brand, and Illuminati II, his luxurious fabric brand that supplies the highest quality cotton fabrics to Noir and other luxury brands under the umbrella of the United Nation's Global Compact principles (www. unglobalcompact.org) and the International Labour Organization (www.ilo.org). 'Illuminati II's vision is to deliver organic and fair trade cotton fabrics whilst ensuring sustainability of the Humane Business Model from the heart of Africa.'

Peter manufactures the Illuminati II cotton fabric in Europe, using raw cotton sourced from Uganda. Peter pays above industry prices for the raw cotton in an attempt to revive the industry and to create sustainable economic growth in the region. He has established the Noir Foundation, which uses a percentage of earnings to fund essential medicine and micro loans. As a result, 'Noir is able to offer collections for both consumer fashion and social

conscience by creating meaningfulness in the luxury segment.' He is adamant that 'it's not more expensive to create beautiful, ethically correct clothing; it's just a lot more hassle, and if you take an ethical approach you need a different supply chain. But, fundamentally, you can't persuade people to join in the ethical challenge unless you give them really sexy, stylish clothes.'

The first Noir collection had a total of 60 pieces and was funded out of Peter's own pocket. Having targeted the luxury end of the market, key price points included trouser suits at €1,150, cotton shirts at €230, silk blouses at €390 and dresses at €850. After the initial success of the first season, Peter was able to attract investment into the business to help it grow and says it has taken three years to break even. Peter says that 'investment is a must if you want to match your ambitions with your growth'. He believes that a certain amount of novelty and hype helped to achieve Noir's initial success, but also says the people he works with and his motivation to make a difference have played an enormous part. He sees the ability to be strategic and position your brand, together with financial acumen and networking skills, as essential to running a successful fashion label.

'Noir is sophisticated, edgy, sexy, luxurious and stands for corporate social responsibility, and these key messages need to be transmitted to the end consumer via the media.' In order to achieve this, the Noir collection, high-quality Noir images, a press show and the Noir story are carefully crafted to allow for media awareness, which can ultimately be translated into business opportunities. Peter explains: 'Noir secured a four-page article in US *Harper's Bazaar* before even hitting the stores. This strong support gave immediate credibility to the brand and enabled Noir to attract retailers.'

Noir offers high-end luxurious designs that are style-driven but underpinned with a socially responsible message.

*W*hat is it that makes being your own boss so attractive and how can you make sure that you are in the best position, before you start spending money, to overcome any obstacles that will be thrown your way? This chapter examines some of the main benefits of setting up on your own as well as looking at the first steps you should consider undertaking. It also looks at the benefits of setting objectives to help you achieve your ultimate goal of running your own fashion label.

Going Solo

Why is it that so many people have the same dream of packing in their nine-to-five job for the dream of setting up their own business?

1 **Freedom:** You're the boss. That means you set the rules. No more asking permission for time off and, more importantly, the freedom to set your own goals.

2 **Creativity/vision:** The opportunity to develop something from scratch exactly as you envisage it, and the possibility of creating a lasting legacy.

3 **Control:** The final word is yours and the success of the venture lies in your hands.

4 **Choice:** Mac or PC, nine-to-five or ten-to-six, orange or white walls: your own taste and style can dictate those of the company.

5 **Ambition:** Your company can be as big as you are able to make it; however, if you want to stay small, you can.

6 **Financial:** There is no ceiling on your potential earnings.

7 **Working from home:** Many new small fashion labels are set up from home. That means no more wasted time commuting.

8 **Choice of personnel:** You can hire the people you want to work with.

9 **Long holidays:** You can take as much time off as you want, whenever you want.

10 **Flexibility:** Your great ideas can be implemented whenever you think they're ready.

Peter Ingwersen from Noir

Although these are common reasons for setting up your own business, for every positive there is a negative, and you need to think about these just as carefully. They include:

1   **Lack of support:** Often you have no-one to turn to when questions arise that are beyond your experience. Lack of support can be a real issue, especially in the early days, when finances may not permit full- or even part-time employees.

2   **The buck stops with you:** You're the boss and the company's success will initially be down to the decisions you make and the work you put in. Your company is therefore only as strong as the skills you bring to the table.

3   **Financial insecurity:** When suppliers are demanding payment and there is only a limited amount in the bank you will be the last to get paid. If the venture fails, any financial investment you have put in will be lost.

4   **Working 24/7:** Your business becomes a full-time venture even when you're not at the studio. Switching off can be very difficult when there is so much to do.

5   **Stress:** Running your own business, especially one as demanding as a fashion label, can be extremely stressful.

6   **Loneliness:** Setting up your own business, particularly if you are working alone from home, can be isolating. If you are used to working in a business environment, being on your own can be a shock to the system.

7   **Lack of motivation:** The only boss checking over your shoulder to make sure you are meeting your targets will be you. If you are not a self-starter, deadlines can quickly slip and problems with your business will arise.

8   **Swapping one boss for many:** Although you may technically be the boss of the company you are still answerable to your customer base. In effect, you may be substituting one boss for many!

==

QUICK TASK Take 5 minutes

Make a list of all the positives you can think of for setting up your own fashion label and then a list of all the negatives. Do the positives outweigh the negatives?

==

Before Setting up in Business

Once you have decided that being your own boss is definitely what you want to do, you need to start focusing your ideas. Here are ten things to think about right from the start. You should give careful consideration to each. They will also be discussed in more detail on the following pages.

1 **Assess yourself:** You are the key to the success of the business. What are your strengths and what areas do you need to develop? Ask others what they think your strengths are.

==

QUICK TASK Take 5 minutes

Make a list of all the key attributes/personality traits you think are needed to be a successful entrepreneur. Assess yourself against this list. How many attributes do you think you possess? Now give the list to a friend or family member and see how they assess you against it.

==

2 **Have a word:** Talk to as many people as you can to get advice. Speak with other business owners and find out what their experiences have been. The more aware you are of the challenges ahead, the better you can prepare.

3 **Make sure there is a business opportunity:** The quickest way to fail is to have a product or service that nobody wants!

==

QUICK TASK Take 10 minutes

Do a SWOT analysis (see page 100) – take your business idea and make a list of all the strengths, weaknesses, opportunities and threats surrounding it. Weigh up the positives against the negatives to establish if it's really as good an idea as you first thought.

==

4 **Research the market:** Just because you think your idea is great doesn't mean others will. You need to research your potential customers' needs and wants as well as their spending habits.

5 **Get relevant experience:** If you want to open a retail store, then work for one first. How will you know what the demands of the fashion and lifestyle sector will be if you've never worked in that arena? It can also give you an understanding of how store buyers plan their seasonal spending budgets and source new labels.

6 **Put it down in a plan:** Keep a notepad with you at all times. Write down any great ideas or potential obstacles. You can start to formulate your ideas and bring to life what's in your head. Eventually this can be developed into a more structured business plan.

7 **Build relationships:** Building strong and lasting relationships is essential for any business. Start early, especially with your bank. Get them on your side. Belief in you and your idea now will help when cash flow gets tight later. You will also need to start thinking about how you can start to build a relationship with your customer base.

8 **Get support:** It is imperative to get the support of friends and family around you. They need to understand the demands placed on your time. Their

support will be crucial, especially when the going gets tough. You will also need specialist support for your fashion business, ranging from pattern cutters to printers, and from stylists to photographers. Start developing this base early so that when the need arises you don't waste precious time searching for the right person.

9   *Seek professional advice:* You will need a good solicitor and accountant. Take time to find them and make sure they are small business specialists. Their professional advice can be the difference between success and failure.

10   *Remember – money in, usually less; money out, always more:* It is quite common for new business owners to overestimate their projected income and underestimate costs. While being optimistic is part and parcel of being an entrepreneur, being prudent when making your initial forecast may save your blushes later.

Setting Objectives

Setting specific objectives will help focus your business idea and allow you to plan your activities. When drawing up your list – or even when thinking about going solo – some of your objectives will be personal (wanting a better standard of living, freedom of expression or more money), whilst others will be business-oriented (getting your product in the pages of a leading magazine, stocking in five major stores during your first season or turning over a set figure in the first year). It is important to distinguish between the two when assessing your priorities for the business, as your objectives may sometimes be in conflict with each other. A personal objective of wanting to spend more time with your family may be in direct conflict with a business objective of looking for the company to break even within the first 18 months, since it is very likely that this will necessitate working extremely long hours. Be aware at the beginning of exactly what you want to achieve.

Before you start setting out your objectives you need to understand the difference between an objective and a goal. Goals are somewhat vague general directions that are not specific enough to be measured, such as 'I want to be the best fashion designer in the world.' Try to avoid setting goals.

Objectives, on the other hand, are specific. They can be output objectives, or they can be attitudinal or behavioural. But, most of all, they are measurable and concise. You can touch an object; it's there, it's actual and it's finite. 'I want to be selected designer of the year by *Vogue* magazine.' Try to set objectives and write them down. The act of writing them down puts in place the plan for their achievement.

Being your own boss is not for everyone and there are many factors to consider before taking the plunge. However, for the many who take this path the positives usually outweigh the negatives and it's a choice they wished they had made sooner. The case studies throughout the book show that for most people, setting up their own label was something they knew they just had to do.

===

TASK Give yourself 30 to 40 minutes to complete steps 1 to 6

STEP 1: *Take an A4 sheet of paper and draw a vertical line down the centre. On the left side write the heading **Personal Objectives**, and on the right side the heading **Business Objectives**. At the very top, in the centre, write the heading **Immediate Objectives**.*

STEP 2: *Take ten minutes to list as many personal objectives as you can think of and write them in the left-hand column. Remember, personal objectives are to do with achieving the lifestyle you want.*

STEP 3: *Take another ten minutes to do the same for your business objectives and write these down in the right-hand column. Remember that these objectives are directed at the way you want the business to develop, for example to pick up five key stockists in your first season, or to employ a design assistant to free up your time for other areas of the business.*

STEP 4: *See if there are any conflicts between your personal and business objectives, or even between objectives on the same list. Ideally, your business objectives should support your personal ones.*

STEP 5: *Choose three personal objectives and two business ones, and try to develop them in more detail. Write them down in the first person future tense – 'I will achieve…'. Make sure you include a date by which each objective will be achieved.*

STEP 6: *Take a separate piece of paper and print each statement of intent in order of priority.*

STEP 7: *When you wake up in the morning read your list aloud, then close your eyes and picture the achievement of each objective. Imagine the feeling of seeing your collection hanging on the rails of your first stockist, taking a bow at the end of your first catwalk show or relaxing on a Caribbean island. Then put the list away and go about your daily business with confidence.*

STEP 8: *Every time you achieve an objective, tick it off your list and take some time to acknowledge your achievement. Replace the objective achieved with a new one and write out a fresh list. Continue the process.*

Immediate Objectives

Personal Objectives	Business Objectives
Better standard of living	Gain five stockists in first season
Freedom of expression	Get product featured in key magazines
Better income	Break even after one year of trading
etc.	etc.

It is important that the list should not be shown to anyone unless they are working with you directly to help you meet your objectives. Achieving your objectives will mean focus and hard work and you can do without the pressure of having others assessing you on what you have and have not achieved to date. By writing down your objectives and visualising them being achieved, you will begin to find that ideas for fulfilling them will simply come to you. When they do, act on them at once. You will find yourself moving towards running the type of fashion business you imagined.

===

Case Study: Knomo

Howard Harrison (former lawyer and investment banker), Benoit Rescue (former creative director in advertising) and Alastair Hops (former retail banker) set up Knomo in October 2004, specialising in luxurious and stylish workbags and accessories for urban professionals. Howard explains: 'The idea for the brand came about after travelling with the standard, ugly black laptop bags and having my bag mistaken for someone else's at Heathrow Airport. I realised there was a gap in the market for a stylish, fashion-led laptop bag and so Knomo was born.'

Knomo launched with six initial styles and a total range of 18 pieces, focusing on leather laptop bags that offered functionality while not sacrificing style. Since then the company has grown rapidly and the product range has expanded to offer a wide range of men's and women's bags and laptop cases as well as small accessories, including iPod covers. Retail price points range from £26 to £250.

The business was self-financed for the first three years with the directors each making an initial investment to get the business off the ground and deciding not to take anything out of the company for the first two years of operation. They were able to further finance the company by securing an overdraft from their bank, as well as a loan through the government-backed Small Business Loan Scheme. Cash flow was further eased by applying for debt funding in the form of trade (import) and invoice finance. Alastair warns, 'Manage your cash flow carefully as cash is king, and make sure you have a friendly and understanding banker.'

It took Knomo 15 months of trading to break even, and they believe their website (*www.knomo.com*) has been an important contributor to the total revenues of the business. The decision to reinvest all funds back into the business in order to grow it internationally means they do not expect any profits in the next two to three years.

They had a very focused sales strategy for the domestic UK market and for introducing the brand globally. 'In the UK we have followed a wholesale model and were very targeted with the retailers that we wanted to stock Knomo and approached retailers directly (not through a trade show). In the first 12 months we listed Knomo at all premium department stores in the UK except for Harrods, which was added in 2006. We have not to date marketed ourselves aggressively to independent retailers and boutiques.'

Within the first 18 months they took the product to trade shows in France and Germany but say that this proved to be too early for the brand. In their second year they started to work with distributors in key overseas markets and believe they have had about a 50 per cent success rate with their distribution partners. They also recognised that the US represented the largest market for their type of product and spent 12 months researching how they could enter it successfully. Having met a number of potential distribution partners and considered launching in the US on their own, they decided the best option would be to form a joint venture with an experienced US partner. Howard says, 'We have recently established a joint venture in the United States and have taken some investors on board to fund this business. We license the product to this joint venture and have a 50 per cent share in the business.'

Knowing when to work with and listen to others, and an ability to network has been of vital importance to Knomo. 'With no experience in the sector, we have learnt a great deal from listening to experts in the industry, retailers and consumers.' Their tip for successful networking is 'always make an effort to speak to as many people as possible, ask lots of questions and have fun!'

This ability to network has been combined with a truly innovative product, and Knomo consider that these are the two main reasons for their brand's success so far. They believe it is essential to make sure you have a USP (unique selling point): 'If you don't stand out you will never get noticed. We have managed to combine clever design with innovative functionality. Without great product, there is no business.' Ultimately they are looking to 'create a global brand that is fun, distinctive and synonymous with cool workbags', and are driven by a 'passion for creating great products and the challenge of re-inventing a sector that is traditionally staid and boring'.

Starting with designer laptop cases, Knomo have gradually increased their product range as the business has expanded

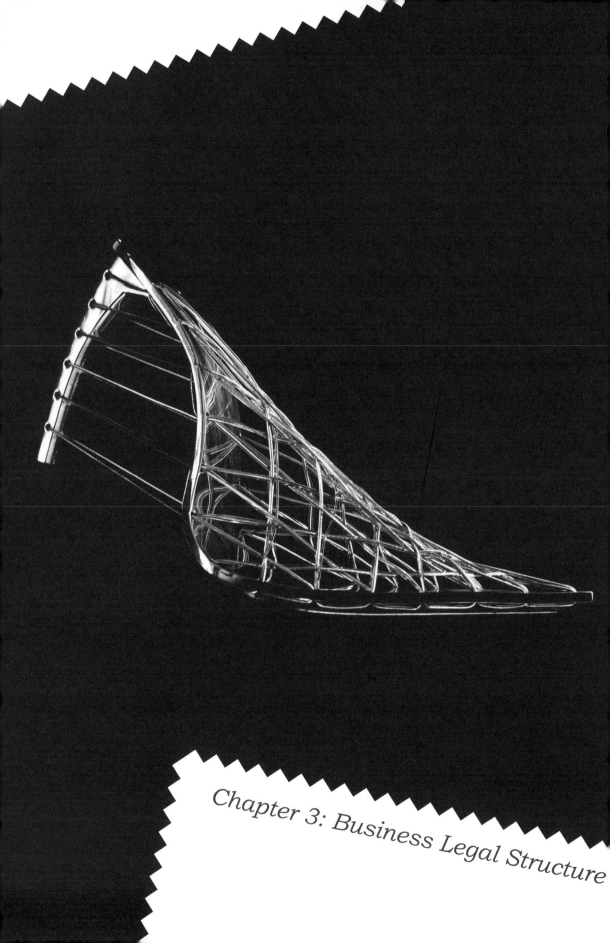

Chapter 3: Business Legal Structure

*F*rom the outset you will need to consider what type of legal structure your business will take.

When deciding, you will have to consider a number of factors. Will you be setting up alone or will you have partners? Will your business require substantial investment to get it off the ground? Setting up in the right way will keep costs to a minimum. It can also help prevent your working relationships turning sour, one of the major causes of business failure.

Not all business structures are appropriate for everyone. Discuss the options with your solicitor, bearing in mind that the structure can be altered later as the business develops and you become more aware of its capabilities and limitations.

Sole Trader

If you are setting up your fashion label on your own, being a sole trader is by far the simplest way to run your business, and does not involve any registration fees. Maintaining records and accounts is straightforward and, as you are operating alone, any profits are yours to keep. On the downside, however, you will be personally responsible for any debts incurred by the business, so if you need a lot of outside investment this might be a risky option.

How to Set Up
In order to set up your business as a sole trader you will need to register yourself as self-employed. This is achieved by visiting the HM Revenue & Customs website and completing form CWF1 (*www.hmrc.gov.uk*).

Management and Raising Finance
As a sole trader you are the business, which means you will make all the decisions on how it will run on a day-to-day basis. Most sole traders will inject some of their own finance into the initial set-up of the business, with further loans from banks or other lenders if and when required.

*Conceptual shoe by
Gil Carvalho*

Keeping Records and Accounts

Sole traders are self-employed and have to make an annual self-assessment tax return to HMRC. You will need to keep records showing your business income and expenses to prove that your annual accounts are correct and that you are paying the correct amount of Income Tax and National Insurance. Your accountant will be able to help if book-keeping and accounts are not your strong point.

Profits, Tax and National Insurance

All profits that the company makes are yours. However, as you are self-employed, your profits are taxed as income. You will also have to pay fixed-rate Class 2 National Insurance contributions and Class 4 National Insurance contributions on your profits.

Liability

As a sole trader you will be personally responsible for any debts. If your label gets into financial difficulty and is unable to meet its repayment obligations your assets, including your home, may be at risk.

Partnership

If you will be joining forces with one or more people, you may find that a partnership is the most flexible and simple way to structure the business. You and your partners will share the costs, risks and liabilities of being in business as well as sharing in the profits. Partners usually share all management decisions and need each other's agreement for all business expenditure.

Partnerships have no legal existence outside of the individual partners themselves, so if one partner resigns, goes bankrupt or dies, then the partnership ceases to exist and must be dissolved. However, it does not necessarily mean the business has to cease trading.

How to Set Up

Draw up a partnership agreement. Page 35 gives an overview of what should be included in a partnership agreement – your solicitor will be able to advise you specifically, based on your circumstances. If you choose not to draw up an agreement you may find yourselves ill-equipped to settle conflicts, allowing minor misunderstandings to escalate into full-blown disputes.

Management and Raising Finance

It is most common for the partners to manage the business, although it is acceptable for you to delegate responsibilities to employees. Most partnerships raise initial start-up funds for the business out of their own personal assets, and then top up with loans as and when required. It is also common to have 'silent' or 'sleeping' partners within this business structure, whereby a partner may contribute money to the business but has no day-to-day involvement.

Keeping Records and Accounts

Each partner is responsible for registering as self-employed and for making their annual self-assessment returns to HMRC. The partnership must therefore keep records of business income and expenses.

Profits, Tax and National Insurance

All profits the company makes are to be shared among the partners. Each partner is then liable for Income Tax on their share of the profits and must also pay fixed-rate Class 2 National Insurance contributions and Class 4 National Insurance contributions.

Liability

Each partner is jointly liable for debts incurred by the business and is equally responsible for paying off the whole debt. In England, Wales and Northern Ireland, partners are not severally liable (each partner being responsible for paying off the entire debt), but in Scotland partners are both jointly and severally liable.

Limited Liability Partnership (LLP)

Limited Liability Partnerships (LLPs) are similar to ordinary partnerships. A number of individuals or limited companies share in the risks, costs, responsibilities and profits of the business.

The main difference between the two is that in an LLP, liability is limited to the amount of money each individual or limited company has invested in the business and to any personal guarantees they have given to raise finance. It is a good option for any 'silent' or 'sleeping' partners who, although investing money, are not involved in making decisions that might result in the failure of the business and want some protection from mismanagement by their partners.

How to Set Up

LLPs, unlike sole traders and partnerships, must be registered with Companies House to come into existence. Although there is no limit to the number of partners within this business structure, at least two must be registered as designated members, which means they have extra legal responsibilities (see *www.companieshouse.gov.uk*). Again, it is strongly recommended that a written agreement be drawn up.

Management and Raising Finance

It is typical for partners to manage the business. Money is raised through individual partners investing their own money and/or through external loans.

Records and Accounts

Your LLP and each individual partner will have to make an annual self-assessment return to HMRC. The business accounts must also be filed annually with Companies House. An annual return (form LLP363) will automatically be sent to the partners before the anniversary of incorporation each year. It must be completed and returned to Companies House with the appropriate fee.

Profits, Tax and National Insurance

Unless otherwise agreed beforehand, each partner takes an equal share of the profits of the business. The individual partners are taxed on their share of profits, and pay Income Tax and National Insurance according to their business structure. So, if one partner in the business is an individual and the other a limited company, then the individual will pay Income Tax and National Insurance contributions, whereas the limited company partner will pay Corporation Tax.

Limited Liability Companies

The most common business structure for UK-based fashion labels is that of a limited company – a company that exists in its own right and whose finances are separated from the personal finances of its owners.

The owners of the company are known as 'shareholders' and may be individuals or other companies. They are not liable for the debts incurred by the business unless they have given guarantees in order to access external funding. Personal savings invested into the company can also be lost if the company fails.

There are several types of limited company:

Designer accessory label Knomo set up as a Limited Liability Company and has three directors

✖ ***Private limited companies:*** These can have one or more members, for example shareholders. They cannot offer shares to the public.

✖ ***Public Limited Companies (PLCs):*** must have at least two shareholders and can offer shares to the public. A PLC must have issued shares to a value of at least £50,000 before it can trade.

✖ ***Private unlimited companies:*** These are rare and usually created for specific reasons. It is recommended that you take legal advice before creating one.

How to Set Up

Limited companies must be registered (incorporated) at Companies House and have at least one director (two for PLCs). From October 2008, it will no longer be necessary for private limited companies to have a company secretary. In a PLC, the company secretary must be professionally qualified. Company directors and secretaries can both be shareholders in the company.

Management and Raising Finance

Either one director, or a board of directors who make all the management decisions, undertakes the day-to-day running of the company. Funding typically comes from initial investment from shareholders, borrowing from external sources and retained profits being pumped back into the business.

Public Limited Companies can also raise money by selling shares on the stock market, but private limited companies cannot.

Records and Accounts

Accounts must be filed annually with Companies House. You will be sent an annual return (form 363s) before the anniversary of incorporation each year. This will need to be checked and any changes made before being returned to Companies House with the appropriate fee.

The directors and secretary are responsible for notifying Companies House of changes in the structure and management of the business.

Profits, Tax and National Insurance

Profits earned by the business are usually either distributed to the shareholders of the business in the form of dividends, or retained within the business to act as working capital. This is usually at the discretion of the director or board of directors.

Limited companies make an annual return to HMRC and are liable to pay Corporation Tax on any reported profits.

Company directors are employees of the company and must pay Class 1 National Insurance as well as Income Tax. The company pays additional National Insurance as a percentage of each employee's salary.

Liability

Shareholders of the business are not personally responsible for the company's debts, but directors who have been asked to give personal guarantees on money borrowed may well be.

Other Business Structures

Franchises

If you are looking to buy into the success of an already established business, then a franchise might well be for you. As the franchisee you will buy a licence to use the name, products, services and management support systems of the franchising company. The licence usually covers a particular geographical area and has a limited lifespan, after which it may be renewable. A franchising company will look at your potential for growth within your geographical region and at your expertise and management skills before deciding whether you are suitable.

Social Enterprises

If your fashion business is driven by a social objective rather than profit, a social enterprise may be best suited to help meet your targets. In a social enterprise all surpluses are reinvested in the business to help meet the social objectives rather than being handed out to shareholders and owners. There is, however, some debate over exactly what constitutes a social enterprise; if you are unsure whether or not your idea could be considered one, go to *www. socialenterprise.co.uk* for further guidance.

Your fashion business will certainly need to be distinguished by its social aims in order to meet the requirements. In certain regions of the UK the Social Enterprise Mark can be applied for, allowing you to show customers that you are hoping to achieve a social outcome (*www.rise-sw.co.uk/socialenterprise*).

Remember:

Seek professional advice if you are unsure which legal structure best suits your needs. Your accountant and solicitor will be able to advise you on all the pros and cons. You may start as a sole trader or under a partnership agreement, but as the need for outside investment surfaces, you might register as a limited company to give your personal assets some protection from the debts incurred by the business.

Partnership Agreements

===

What to include:

- ✖ **Name of the partnership:** *Agree on a name for your partnership. You can use your own last names, such as Smith & Jones, or you can adopt and register a business name that ties in with the product and image you hope to sell. The partnership name does not have to be the name that your business will trade under and you might actually decide to create a number of different sub-brands under your partnership each with a different brand name.*

- ✖ **Contributions to the partnership:** *Work out and record from the outset who is contributing what in terms of cash, property or services, as well as the percentage to which each partner is entitled.*

- ✖ **Allocation of profits, losses and draws:** *Determine whether profits and losses will be allocated in proportion to each partner's percentage interest in the business. Decide how profit will be drawn (on a regular monthly basis or annually).*

- ✖ **Partners' authority:** *Decide if you will require the consent of one or all of the partners before making any contracts that legally bind the partnership.*

- ✖ **Partnership decision-making:** *Will you require a unanimous vote from all the partners for every business decision that is to be made or will you offer a little more freedom, with a unanimous vote required only for major decisions, leaving partners free to make minor decisions?*

- ✖ **Management duties:** *Whose job is it to do what? Look at the management needs of your partnership as well as the natural strengths each partner brings to the table. Allow partners to work to their strengths and divide up the major responsibilities fairly.*

- ✖ **Admitting new partners:** *At some point you may want to expand the business by bringing in investment and new partners. Work out a procedure at the outset so that all partners are happy with potential plans for growth.*

- ✖ **Withdrawal of a partner:** *Try to agree an acceptable buyout strategy in the event that one partner decides to leave the business. This will reduce the risk of relationships turning sour later.*

- ✖ **Resolving disputes:** *Rather than going straight to court if you and your partners become deadlocked on an issue, you might want to agree an alternative dispute resolution from the outset. This could include mediation or arbitration.*

Dealing with these issues from the outset will ensure sure that all the partners understand the expectations placed on them and have agreed to the rules governing the settlement of any disputes. It is highly recommended that you work with your solicitor to make sure the agreement covers all areas of concern.

===

Case Study: Ed Hardy

Born in Avignon in southern France, Christian Audigier was drawn to the rock-and-roll lifestyle, and looked to fashion as a means of expressing his vision to the world. He launched the Ed Hardy clothing line in January 2006, a collection inspired by the youth of America, vintage-inspired fashion, Hollywood stardom and motorcycle and tattoo culture – most importantly the artwork of Don Ed Hardy, the 'godfather of tattoo'.

At 19 Christian was dubbed the 'King of Jeans' by *Sportswear International* magazine for his creative design work, elaborate parties and his unprecedented denim museum in Paris, which paid homage to some of his favourite stars, including Elvis Presley and Steve McQueen. He moved to the US at a very young age, setting up his own freelance consultancy and working with Levi's, Diesel, American Eagle Outfitters, NafNaf and Lee, among others. However it was when he joined the clothing company Von Dutch that he gained international credibility, transforming the relatively unknown brand into a global one.

After his success at Von Dutch he was looking for a new challenge. 'I was looking at all these people on the street with tattoos in California, and thought, "Why not do a T-shirt with tattoos?"' He started doing research on tattoo artists and Don Ed Hardy's name kept coming up. 'I wasn't even sure if he was alive or not. I contacted him and he called me back and here we are today.'

Christian persuaded Don Ed Hardy to grant him exclusive rights to the Don Ed Hardy back catalogue of tattoo designs to put on clothing for worldwide distribution, using his name to promote the line. He bought all of Hardy's archives so that he could start a new phenomenon. Three years after Von Dutch, and taking the strategy that had worked so well for him there, Christian set about developing a global brand.

The cleverly designed T-shirts, denim and accessories reflect Christian's own fast-paced lifestyle and passion for colour. He started to develop the brand further by signing the Ed Hardy motorcycle manufacturing deal, producing and distributing the collectible Ed Hardy energy drink and launching his own retail stores. He constantly looks for opportunities to expand the Ed Hardy product portfolio, reasoning that the brand is more

than a brand – 'It's a lifestyle. It's something that people want to be a part of.'

Christian has always had a charismatic and colourful approach to fashion and uses an ebullient promotional strategy to good effect. While the product has been integral to the success of each of the brands he has developed, Christian believes that his ability to get the right people and, in particular, the right celebrities wearing it has been paramount.

Britney Spears was one of Christian's first celebrity clients when he was at Von Dutch. 'I put a cap on her, and another one on Justin Timberlake. At the time they had split up. They were in all the magazines, all around the world, sporting the Von Dutch cap. This is how a phenomenon starts.' Since then he has worked hard to develop what is believed to be one of the best little black books of Hollywood A-listers in the fashion industry, with a client base that includes Jessica Alba, Mariah Carey, Mickey Rourke, Paris Hilton, Snoop Dogg, Chris Brown, Usher, Marilyn Manson, Madonna, Shakira, Ciara, Heidi Klum and Jamie Foxx.

Christian says, 'You've got to market the product!' and getting the product on the right people is key. 'I follow the same rules as I always have – taking care of my friends and celebrities, sending them my stuff and inviting them over.' He recognises that the paparazzi play a huge role in the promotion of his brand and that the reported bad behaviour of celebrities can often play into the rock-and-roll lifestyle reflected by the Ed Hardy brand. 'The people fighting, or getting pregnant, or being drunk or on drugs, suddenly it's on CNN. That is good advertising for me. Gossip and the internet are really important today.'

Christian has gone on to launch the Christian Audigier line and another clothing line, SMET. All three are sold globally through a network of distributors in over 40 countries and in over 20 branded Ed Hardy and Christian Audigier licensed stores outside the US. Revenues of Audigier's companies have grown from $10 million in 2005 to over $35 million in 2006 and over $80 million in 2007.

Christian Audigier bought the rights to tattoo artist Don Ed Hardy's artwork, initially putting them on to T-shirts and caps before expanding the brand across a number of different product categories

Chapter 4: What's in a Name?

A great name is the beginning of a great brand. The best name for your brand is one that customers can easily remember and associate with you. Your brand name can also be protected as a trademark. In the fashion industry it is particularly important to get your name and logo right, as they are such an integral part of creating your overall brand image. This chapter will take you through the process of choosing a name and designing your logo. Before you begin, however, it is important to understand that you need to consider at least two, and possibly three, names for your company. The first is the brand name, also known as the 'mark', 'label' or source 'identifier'. The second is the trade name, the name under which the business is conducted and is applicable if the business is incorporated in some way (see Chapter 3). Finally, the third is the domain name, which is used for your website on the internet.

Brand Name

The brand name is an identifier for your product and is by far the most important of the three names. It is the 'mark' used to distinguish your product from those of another business so that consumers are not confused. Your choice of name is important for many reasons:

✖ Quite often it is the first thing your customers come in contact with

✖ Your name is your most visible attribute

✖ It will be the cornerstone of all your marketing materials, from the storefront, to carrier bags, swing tickets and lookbooks

✖ Your name portrays your label's personality, so you want it to stand out and be easily memorised.

The first step is to look at the competition and see if there are any trends that you should be taking into consideration. It is very common for high-end luxury designers to use their own names, as they are the main focus behind the label. Think Marc Jacobs, John Galliano, Alexander McQueen. Each time you buy a piece from these collections you buy a piece of the designer's creativity and the name reflects this added value. By way of contrast, at the high-street retail end of the market we have Gap, French Connection, Diesel, Miss Sixty. They tell us little about the designers behind the brand, but with effective marketing and

Ed Hardy stand at trade show Bread & Butter

advertising campaigns they have become easily remembered and reflect the type of product and the brand's personality.

The most effective names are often those that reflect the personalities of the business and its people – even if they don't describe exactly what the brand stands for. You therefore need to identify what type of image you want your brand or product to project – for example exclusive, accessible, feminine, masculine, sporty, edgy.

✖ Do you want the name to reflect what your business produces – clothing, accessories, jewellery, etc.? Or would something more abstract be suitable?

✖ Do you want to use your own name, linking your own personality and image intrinsically with that of your label? It's worth considering here that if there is potential for investors to buy out your company, and with it your brand name, it will leave you without control of your own name in the marketplace (examples include Roland Mouret, Jimmy Choo and Jill Sander) (see Trade Name, page 42). It is possible to have expensive legal fights between persons of the same name in the fashion industry.

✖ Do you want a traditional-sounding name, conveying durability and old-fashioned values, or a modern name, suggesting a fresh, innovative approach?

✖ Try to make the name instantly memorable, easy to remember, and relevant to your product.

Marks have been classified by the courts into a hierarchy of four categories: generic, descriptive, suggestive, and arbitrary or fanciful. Generic terms and/or generic uses, for example 'jeans' as a mark for jeans, should be avoided as they are not distinctive and either needed for use by others in the trade or widely used by them. Descriptive terms may, by use and advertising over time, become distinctive but this may never overcome the right of third parties to make fair, descriptive use of the word or words in question – even in a globalized world market you should expect to find markedly different treatment at the hands of trademark examiners in different countries as to what is generic or merely descriptive, the United States being quite strict. Suggestive marks are distinctive if they only 'suggest' rather than describe a characteristic of your product. Fanciful and arbitrary marks are the strongest.

Some important don'ts are:

✖ Don't make a brand name or identifier generic: for example, don't say 'care for your guccis' when you mean a pair of Gucci shoes. There are plenty of others who will make use of brand names for various purposes, good or bad, so the brand owner, if no one else, should insist on good brand usage wherever he or she can. If you don't have a generic name for a branded product, invent one – VELCRO is for 'hook and loop fasteners' (a reference to the two woven tapes, one with looped pile and one with loops which are cut so that they hook into the pile).

✖ Don't adopt as a brand name anything which is arguably immoral or scandalous, deceptive, or deceptively misdescriptive, or which disparages, falsely suggests a connection with or sponsorship by another person, or

The name you choose for your fashion label will be extremely important and will be used across a number of different mediums, including bags. Take the time to get the right name for your business

brings a person or institution or religious belief or national insignia into contempt or disrepute.

✖ Don't omit to get written permission to use the name of a living person.

✖ Think about the future and don't use words or phrases that are likely to date quickly.

✖ If you're likely to be trading overseas, check that the name doesn't mean anything inappropriate in the languages of your target audience.

✖ Think about callers and customers and don't use very long names, strange wordings and unusual spelling, or names that are hard to pronounce.

✖ Don't confuse a brand name with a trade name or domain name – see below.

Protecting Your Brand Name

Once you have chosen your name, you need to register it as a trademark to prevent others using the name, for example to name a new product or service. First you need to check that it isn't too similar to one that someone is using as a trademark. Even if you don't choose to register it as a trademark now, it may also save you a lot of time and hassle in the future. Find out whether someone has already registered it by visiting the Patent Office website (for details see end of book).

Registering your brand name can also be undertaken on the Patent Office Website. It costs around £200 to register in one class of goods or service, and a further £50 for each subsequent class (there are 34 classes of goods but only a few will be directly linked with fashion). The process of registering a trademark can take anywhere up to six months to finalise, quite often longer.

Trade Name

This is the name under which your business is run. In the sole trader structure (page 29), a brand name and the name of the business or trade name might easily be the same. It is advisable, however, to adopt a form of business which offers some protection from unlimited liability. In this case the brand name and the trade name will be legally separate things even though it is usually the case that the business entity will own the brand name as part of its assets.

For Knomo, choosing a name was not an easy task. Benoit Rescue explains, 'We tried to think about what the brand would represent, whilst also thinking of something original for a technology-related accessories brand. "Knomo", a combination of "knowledge" and "mobility", seemed to fit the bill as, despite being a little unusual, it seemed people remembered us all the more!'

You may easily incorporate your business in some manner and thus adding Ltd after the name – or even operate under a partnership name – with the result that the name of the business can be presented separately (for example Guccio Gucci S.p.A is the trade name in Europe and Gucci is the brand name). Avoid 'clutter' or confusion between brand name and trade name in advertising and promotion by presenting the brand name in a distinctive manner as a mark and avoid including the trade name. If you have to include the trade name, include it in an entirely separate space on the advert.

Registering Your Trade Name

If you are going to become a limited company you will need to register your name with Companies House. You can either do it online, at a cost of £20, or use a registration agent. When you form your company, you will need to send Companies House a Memorandum of Association which, as well as the name, generally includes the registered address of your firm and an explanation of what it will do. Other information may be necessary, depending on the type of company. This will prevent a company using a similar name to yours, but will not protect your brand name. A properly used brand name which is registered as a mark could be infringed by a similar trade name used by a third party, because when consumers might be confused trademarks can trump trade names, so it is worth registering your brand name as a trademark.

Domain Name

An internet address, or uniform resource locator (URL) may be highly desirable for promotion via the internet. You will almost certainly need to create a website and email address with your company name in it, so check whether the domain name you want to use is available. The best way to protect the domain name from unfair competition from third parties is to make sure that the operative part of the address, the second level domain name between the prefix 'http://www.' and the ending top level domain (TLD) 'com', is identical with a registered mark for the brand name, so that it might be infringement of the mark for a third party to 'knock off' the second level domain name. If your name is taken don't give up – perhaps there is a variation you could use? It is quite common for people to register names in the hope of selling them later for a profit, so you may still be able to buy your chosen name. When registering your domain it is a good idea to buy a number of endings, for example .com, .net, .co.uk, .biz. There are two reasons for this. First, when people try to find your website they might key in any number of variations. This means that you can redirect all the other endings to your site. Second, it prevents other people registering a similar web address.

Remember, your domain name, accessible on the internet, is not the same thing as your brand name or your trade name. It is your brand name that must be registered as your trademark, your trade name which defines the legal entity which is your business, and your domain name which is your electronic address on the internet for information (passive) or for sales (active).

The End Result
You know you have come up with a successful name when a customer looks at your product, hears the name and says 'I get it'. You need your customers to connect with your brand image as quickly as possible. If, from the moment they see your product, name and logo, they understand the story behind the brand and the lifestyle it is projecting then you have made a huge step forward in the success of your business.

Names that are distinctive, memorable and positive will go a long way towards promoting your company or product, so put in the time and effort to find a great one. After all, it is much the same as naming your children. It's something that will be with you for ever.

Overleaf
Logos play a massive part in developing the aesthetic of a brand and sustaining its image

Simplicity when developing logos is often the key for designers delivering product at the high end of the market

Fashion Logos

Although it can be difficult to measure the impact of a logo on the overall success of a fashion business, the right logo is crucial to creating and sustaining a brand image, which is a major contributing factor to the success and profitability of a brand. A good logo should give the potential customer a general perception of the brand's products and services, and add a degree of sophistication, reliability and authenticity.

As a new fashion label you will be fighting to get noticed, so you need to find a balance between capturing your prospective customer's attention and looking like you're trying too hard – or, worse, not trying at all. It is essential to remember your audience, plan for the future and keep it simple. The secret to an inexpensive, but effective logo is simplicity. Your logo is part of your marketing strategy; it is about communication, not just art.

Remember: your image is how people perceive your product and brand, and not just how you want it to be perceived.

Motifs

Motifs are an important element of fashion logos. The motif used should clearly communicate the style of the brand. That's why many fashion labels will just use the company's emblem or initials as motifs on their fashion logos. Examples of such logos include Ralph Lauren, Louis Vuitton, Fred Perry and Adidas.

Fonts

Choosing the right font is critical. A lot of labels choose not to have any branding other than their name. It is the font that creates the design twist and provides distinctiveness, making your logo unique. Just as you did when choosing your company name, decide on the perception you want the customer to have of your brand.

Colour

Fashion logos tend to use high-impact colours like red, black, white or gold. Although you can use any colour, it is important to consider the colour of the background on which the logo will be placed. High-impact colours tend to give a positive look and feel.

===

QUICK TASK Take 10 minutes

Type the name you are considering for your label in any font at 20 point. Copy and paste the name a hundred times on the page and then apply a different font to each. Discard any that you feel are not suited to the brand image you are trying to project. Pin up the remainder on your wall for consideration.

===

Trying to develop your image is a subjective process. It may not be until the business cards are printed, the back labels are stitched in and the swing tickets attached, that you discover that some people love it and others loathe it. That's when you'll know whether it works – or not.

Remember:

Your logo is the creative expression of your brand's identity and one of the strongest marketing tools for communicating your brand ethos to the customer.

Developing Logos

==

Malcolm Crews – *Graphic Designer/Artistic Director, NY*

Before developing your logo you first need to determine:

1 *What your product is. Casual, dress, sportswear, accessories?*
    Female, male, male and female, kids?

2 *Who your customer is. Build a visual of your ideal customer; a symbol of*
    'who' the brand is.

3 *What your price point will be. High end? Moderate? Mass market?*

4 *A point of view (POV). Have a POV for your label and stick to it.*

5 *A brand name that best tells your story. (A designer's name is not always*
    the best option for a brand name.)

Once you have determined these points you can start to develop. Logo design
helps guide prospective customers, who may not initially see the product.
Font, colour and motif can all tell a story.

Aspects to consider when developing a logo:

✖ *Do I want a logo-mark combined with a font treatment? Hire a good graphic*
   designer or art director to help you to develop your logo. Give as much
   information and direction as possible. It really can help to get an outsider's
   take on your vision. It's easy to be 'too close'.

✖ *Do I want a logo motif that can be used separately from the font treatment?*

✖ *Do I want a font treatment only?*

Readability

✖ *Ideally, your logo should be able to stand the test of time.*

✖ *Do you want a modern, retro or classic logo?*

✖ *Serif and sans-serif fonts are an easy way to tell a brand's story and can*
   conjure up different styles to the reader; sans-serif fonts are generally seen as
   'modern, clean, fast', whereas early newspapers and flyers used serif fonts.

Font examples

Before finally deciding on a logo, check:

✖ *Does it convey the brand's image/direction?*
✖ *Is it understandable and readable?*
✖ *Is it timeless?*
✖ *Does it work for various uses: printing, embroidery, positive/negative? Is it legible at various sizes?*

Create a logo standards guide

No matter how simple or complex your logo, a standards guide is important for consistency as your brand grows and you begin to use external suppliers.

```
Logo standards example
```

✖ *Logo color will always be black or tonal.*
✖ *Size of logo, when used in signage or packaging shall never be smaller than half an inch (1.27 cm).*
✖ *When using a logo for marketing/advertising purposes, it will always appear in the bottom right-hand corner, half an inch (1.27 cm) from each edge.*
✖ *Logo should never be seen/used on the exterior of any garment, other than the swing ticket or other marketing materials.*
✖ *Type accompanying logo shall always be Helvetica bold and be no larger than half the logo size, and no smaller than one eighth of the logo size.*

font: Helvetica Inserat Roman

Chapter 5: Working from Home v Setting Up a Studio

*E*stablishing a good and practical working environment is essential to success. While many aspiring designers start off in their bedrooms for practical and financial reasons, there are still certain requirements for a work space. This chapter looks at the pros and cons of working at home against the cost of taking up a studio and examines how your work space may be perceived by buyers and press.

Working From Home

When starting out, keeping costs to a minimum is important to the financial stability of the business. Working from home can be a good way to save money. You will, however, need to weigh up the pros and cons to be sure that it won't actually cost your business in the long run.

Pros and Cons

==

Pros
Not having to commute; saving on rent; taking calls in your pyjamas; getting up at 8:30 am and still being at work for 9:00 am.

Cons
The office can easily overflow into your living space; it can be difficult to 'switch off' during evenings and weekends; there can be distractions from housemates.

==

Do You Have the Right Space?
If you have some space at home from which to work, you need to establish if it is the right space for you.

Work out how much space you will need
This will depend on the type of fashion business you are setting up. If you will be cutting your own patterns and sampling your own product you will need a lot of flat work space. If you will be selling your product directly through your website you will need to have enough storage space for your stock without infringing on the rest of the household. If you will be outsourcing everything, a desk with the bare essentials will suffice.

Allocate a dedicated work space

You should try to allocate a permanent space to your business; ideally a room rather than just a corner. A separate room will reduce the risk of distraction. You should be able to separate your work life from your personal life as much as possible and to shut the door to either as and when required.

Keep it flexible

Will your allocated space give you the flexibility you need? At times it may need to be a design studio, sales showroom, warehouse or distribution centre. The more you can move things around and make the space suit the activity, the better. When you have designated a space for your home office, take measurements so you know exactly how much space you have to play with. Sketch a layout of the room and map out where the furniture and equipment will go.

Get the lighting right

Running your own business will require high levels of energy and enthusiasm. There is nothing more likely to sap these than a badly lit work environment. Bad lighting can cause headaches, eye strain and fatigue. Choose a space with windows that can provide some natural light – you will need good lighting to choose colour palettes for your collections. Lighting the wall behind a computer monitor can reduce eye strain, while a good adjustable desk lamp can provide light in a range of different situations.

Make the right first impression

You work environment says a great deal about you and your business. Giving potential clients a tour of your entire property is not the best starting point so try to keep your office confined to an easily accessible space near the entrance. If your work environment gives the wrong impression, try meeting outside of home as much as possible, and look into hiring meeting or showroom space when needed.

Making Use of the Space

No matter how good a work space you have, you need to make the best use of it.

Be logical

Try to create a work space that will maximise your efficiency and work flow. Know where everything is and keep key functions like phones, computers and sewing machines in your primary work space.

Be tidy

You will need to switch between job functions several times a day, so keep your work space organised. Know where everything is at all times. Labelling can help with this. At the end of each day leave the space ready for the beginning of the next.

Remember storage

Take time to think about your storage requirements. Shelves mounted on the wall provide useful storage for home office supplies and files and do not take up any floor space. You will also require drawers for trims, buttons and fastenings, and clothes rails for your samples.

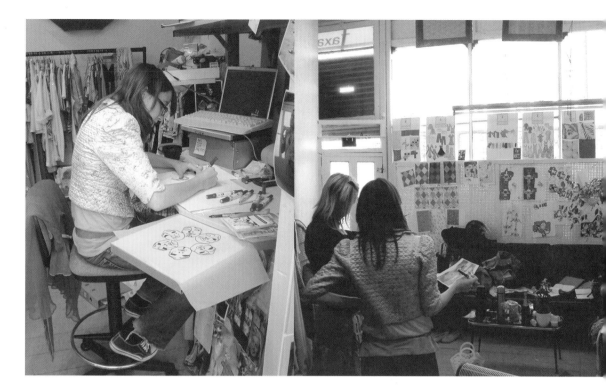

Make sure you have a designated space that will allow you to be both creative and productive. Your surroundings should inspire you

Think multi-functional

When space is an issue, buy furniture and equipment that can perform different purposes. This could include an all-in-one printer, scanner and copier, or a storage cabinet that also provides a work surface. Furniture that can be rolled out of the way is also useful.

Keep trim

Keep any unnecessary items away from your work space. This might include anything likely to distract you (such as televisions) and stop you from working efficiently. However, you will be working in a creative industry, so don't deprive yourself of things that will help to stimulate the creative juices.

The Practicalities

There are certain things to take into account in order to make the arrangement workable.

Legal and insurance

You are legally required to notify your landlord or mortgage lender that you will be working from home, as your property may now be considered semi-commercial, rendering your initial mortgage agreement invalid. There are special semi-commercial mortgages, and your lender may require you to move to one of these. Check your home insurance, as it probably doesn't cover working from home – if you expect to receive business visitors then you will probably need additional cover. Standard working from home insurance coverage can include:

- ✖ Business contents
- ✖ Employers', public and product liability
- ✖ Legal expenses
- ✖ Business interruption protection.

Working from home optional extras can include:

- ✖ Buildings insurance – accidental damage cover for your home business area and your home
- ✖ Home contents insurance – accidental damage cover for your home contents
- ✖ Personal possessions – peace of mind if you take personal items away from home
- ✖ 'All risks' on business equipment – cover for accidental loss or damage of office equipment
- ✖ Computer breakdown – covers breakdown and failure of computer equipment, or loss/damage to computer records.

Source: *www.theaa.com*

It is also worth ensuring that any particularly expensive items of equipment or product are covered. You may be able to include some or all of these in your home contents insurance. You may also want to increase your security measures if there is a great deal of expensive equipment or merchandise being stored. The more security you have, the lower your monthly premium will be.

Health and safety

You will be legally responsible for your own health and safety and that of any employees or visitors to your premises. Study the legislation. There are some simple things you can do to make your space a good one to work in. Make sure your workstation is comfortable, and that any wires or cabling are located in a safe place (to avoid tripping). Take the time to undertake a risk assessment of the premises and identify any potential hazards.

Remember:

Make sure you comply with the law regarding insurance and health and safety regulations. Keep home life and work life separate. If you are living with others, make sure they know when and where you work.

Working from a Studio/Workshop

Taking up a studio, office or workshop space is a big step. However, at some point you will probably need to find yourself a space away from home that will allow you to conduct your business effectively.

Pros and Cons

==

Pros
A flexible work environment; separation of work and home life; a professional business address.

Cons
The cost implications of running the studio; the financial commitment of a lease.

==

Identify Your Requirements
Before you start looking for potential space, make a list of all your requirements. This streamlines the hunt for premises. The key points will be:

Function
Make a list of the key activities of your business. Your prospective space must allow all of these activities to take place. If it is a small space, does it give you the flexibility to move things around to create a different look when customers call?

Location
Think about:
* The length of commute from your home to the studio or to your clients or suppliers
* The journey your customers will have make
* Transport links and access to parking.

Cost
Set a realistic budget and stick to it. It's not just the rent or mortgage you will need to think about, but also:
* Set-up costs for getting the space how you need it to look
* Additional property costs: business rates, services charge and insurance, security deposit
* Day-to-day running costs: gas, water, electricity, telephone, internet and cleaning/maintenance.

Size
Keep things to a minimum. However, don't go too small, and make sure you have enough space to accommodate potential new employees or casual labour as and when required.

Services
Think about the services you will need: toilets and kitchen facilities.

Designer Karen Walker at work in her studio

Isolation

Running your own business can be lonely, so think carefully before choosing a location that cuts you off too much from the outside world, unless that's what inspires you the most.

Security

The most affordable studios are often located in slightly less desirable areas. Think about safety and security.

Types of Space

There are many different types of work space available. Decide which one will suit you best.

Individual work spaces

Often owned by private landlords, these can range from retail premises to offices or industrial workshops. There is often room for negotiation on rent and conditions of the lease.

Professionally managed studios

The monthly fee usually includes all studio expenses from rent, business rates and services to utilities. You will usually be surrounded by creative companies – this can help with inspiration, networking and finding potential suppliers. The security is usually good and administrative functions may be thrown in. Rent, however, tends to be a little higher and you're less likely to find a bargain.

Shared studios

If you have found a fantastic location that ticks all your boxes but is just a bit too big and expensive, you could look for similar businesses to share the space with you. This is sometimes called a 'co-operative'. Have a solicitor draw up a contract for each tenant and draw up a set of studio rules.

Finding a Studio

There are many ways to find a studio.

* �֍ **Word of mouth:** Recommendations from friends and family or people already in the industry.
* ✖ **Business support agencies:** Enterprise agencies' listings.
* ✖ **Estate agents:** Estate agents' commercial listings.
* ✖ **Internet:** Information from agents to business organisations and personal postings.
* ✖ **Managed studios:** Managed premises will often have a waiting list that you can put your name down on.
* ✖ **Advertising:** Ads in local shops and on e-bulletin boards for relevant fashion sites.
* ✖ **Taking a stroll:** Seeing 'for rent' signs on commercial properties; talking to local business owners.

Getting the Space

Once you have found the ideal space, before you put pen to paper and sign the contract, there are some considerations.

* ✖ Negotiate with your landlord: can you get a rent reduction or arrange a rent-free period whilst setting up the studio?
* ✖ Check out your landlord. It's a good idea to speak to other tenants.
* ✖ Get your solicitor to check over the rental agreement. How binding is the contract and for how long are you expected to sign? Can you make it more favourable to you?
* ✖ Check whether you are responsible for service charges, power, water, rates, and so on.

Do your homework and get an idea of the rental values of different types of property in the area.

Chapter 6: Jack-of-All-Trades?

*B*eing your own boss within a small company means multi-tasking. In the fashion industry, in addition to all the day-to-day functions, there are some specialised roles. You need to work out how many of these you can take on and how many you will need to outsource. If you need to bring people in to work for you, you'll need to get up to speed on hiring and firing techniques and legislation. This chapter looks at the functions involved in the supply chain.

The Supply Chain

Taking a fashion product from initial concept to being worn by your potential customers can be complicated, and involves a variety of job functions. The overall process is known as the supply chain (see pages 16–17), and how you manage it will determine how successful your business will be. There are four main steps in the supply chain: researching the market and trends; design development; production; and sales and distribution. Within each of these four steps there are several roles, and within a large organisation an individual will have responsibilities that spread over a number of the steps. The table shows the typical job functions, and where they come into play within the four stages of the supply chain.

Key Job Roles Within the Stages of the Supply Chain

Step 1 Research fashion trends	*Step 2* Design development	*Step 3* Production	*Step 4* Sales and distribution
Fashion forecaster	Designer	Production manager	Sales director
Designer	Buyer	Buyer	Merchandiser
Buyer	Merchandiser	Merchandiser	Allocator/distributor
	Pattern cutter	Designer	PR/Marketing manager
	Sample machinist	Pattern cutter	Fashion photographers/ stylists
	Garment/fabric technologist	Grader	Fashion journalists
		Garment/fabric technologists	Retail managers
		Quality controller	Sales assistants

Image by David Hardy

Each of these functions is essential to delivering the right product at the right price, time, location and quality. You need to identify which of these roles you yourself will be able to take on board and which you may need to outsource. The earlier you can identify the areas in which you will need to bring in support to your business the earlier you can start to work out a realistic start-up figure.

Although some job functions may appear in more than one stage, for ease of reference they have been included below only where they are most involved on a day-to-day basis. For example, although sample machinists may have input at the design development stage, they are most involved in step 3 (Production) and are therefore discussed under this heading.

STEP 1: Research Fashion Trends

Fashion is all about trends. You must understand the trends that affect your target consumer, learn to identify the direction the fashion industry is moving in and develop your product accordingly (see Chapter 8). Large fashion retailers often have a specialist fashion forecaster (such as WGSN or the Donegar Group) working with them or have access to external trend research agencies for up-to-date information.

Fashion forecaster:
- ✖ Shops the market, attends trade and fashion events, researches online trade sites
- ✖ Offers fashion designers guidance on changes in colour, fabric and shape, and analysis of social trends that will affect fashion
- ✖ Combines a knowledge of fashion design and history with consumer information.

STEP 2: Design Development

Based on your research into the market, your customers and the trends that are being predicted you must start to develop your initial product range (see Chapter 9). Whether or not you will be the designer, you will quite often need to look at the product you are developing from a number of different viewpoints. Within a large retail company the designers will work with the buying and merchandising teams to make sure they are creating the best product for the customer. If you are taking on all of these roles yourself you must be able to develop a healthy balance between the artistic role of designer and the role of the merchandiser, who will look at the product from the point of view of the previous season's sales analysis. Avoid falling into the trap of creating a product so elaborate that it has no commercial attraction, or a product based so much on previous seasons' sales that it becomes too safe and does not offer the customer something sufficiently different.

Put yourself in the shoes of the buyers from the stores you aim to sell to and the customers who will wear your product.

Pattern cutters, sample machinists and garment/fabric technologists are also involved at this stage to make sure design specifications can be met.

Designer:

- ✖ Researches trends through comparative shopping, attending fabric fairs and trade shows, as well as following media, music and other social influences
- ✖ Creates storyboards and product ranges
- ✖ Draws up specifications for costings and sampling
- ✖ Sources fabric and trimmings
- ✖ Works with pattern cutters and sample machinists
- ✖ Approves samples
- ✖ Visits manufacturers.

Left
Fashion forecasters will research a number of places including trade shows to find current and future trends

Right
Specification sheets like those shown pinned up in the design room of the fashion brand Schumacher are a key step in the design development of fashion products

Buyer:

* Is responsible for planning the new ranges each season
* Researches trends through comparative shopping and sales analysis
* Holds regular range review meetings with senior management
* Controls the annual budget
* Sets criteria for suppliers, including price
* Ensures deadlines and delivery requirements are met
* Works out lead times to make sure the product is in store in time.

Merchandiser:

* Works alongside the buying team to forecast the next season's ranges from an analysis of the previous season's sales figures
* Helps to decide the product mix to maximise sales
* Ensures that profit margins and stock targets are met
* Is often in charge of a large budget
* Manages the supply chain, checking deliveries and monitoring relationships with suppliers
* Works closely with the distribution team to maximise in-store stock ratios.

Pattern cutter:

* Turns the designer's sketches into patterns from which samples are made – patterns will later be used for production as well
* Establishes a block (the measurements that give a collection a size structure)
* Makes an initial draft of the pattern on paper then develops a toile in fabric, making any adjustments to get the correct fit and look
* Traces the paper patterns on to hard card
* Does pattern cutting by hand or using an automated/computerised Pattern Design System (PDS).

Garment technologist:

* Makes sure that samples from manufacturers fit perfectly and that fabric is of the quality expected
* Uses technical garment-making skills to make suggestions for improvement
* Provides technical support to the buying function
* Works with suppliers to ensure production standards are maintained
* Organises tests of materials and coordinates reports.

STEP 3: Production

Once you enter the realms of producing fashion the process becomes very technical quite quickly. If you are taking on the physical making of your product yourself you will need to have the skills to produce it to a commercial quality. If you are going to outsource your production you will be at a disadvantage when dealing with manufacturers unless you have a production manager to oversee the process.

Given the importance of quality, you cannot afford to waste time and money getting the production process wrong. Having had all the time in the world to develop your first season's samples, you will quickly find that you will be overseeing the production of one season's sales whilst sampling your next season's line. For this reason many small fashion labels find the production

Developing fashion products is a technical process and involves such jobs as pattern cutters (above), sample machinists (top right) and garment technologists (bottom right)

process can be the bane of their lives, so don't be surprised if you spend most of your time acting as the production manager (see Chapter 10).

Production manager:

✖ Is responsible for managing the entire sampling and production process
✖ Ensures that the product comes in on budget and is delivered on time
✖ Sources suppliers if not using in-house facilities, and negotiates prices
✖ Works with the sales team to calculate the quantities needed for production.

Fabric technologist:

✖ Develops and maintains standards for fabric in production
✖ Works with designers to ensure the fabrics meet the needs of the product in terms of quality, performance and price.

Quality control:

✖ Creates internal standards for product quality
✖ Oversees quality procedures
✖ May physically measure garments against specifications to make sure they are correct.

Grader:

✖ Grades patterns to develop a full size-range for each style
✖ Develops a sizing structure
✖ Works with pattern cutters and designers.

Sample machinist:

✖ Is skilled in the use of industrial sewing machines
✖ Makes up the samples from specifications and patterns
✖ Finishes off garments to a high spec.

STEP 4: Sales and Distribution

Once you have researched your market, have an overview of the upcoming season's trends, have designed and sampled your collection and made sure the production capabilities are in place, it's finally time to sell your product line. The roles you will take on yourself here might differ depending on whether or not you have a retail or wholesale business strategy, but whether you sell your range yourself and control your own PR and marketing in-house or use an agent (see Chapter 12), you will need help to create a buzz about you and your line (see Chapter 11). Fashion stylists, photographers and journalists all help create the necessary awareness of your product and brand that helps drive the sales needed to pump money back into your business. Even though these roles will not be internal to your business you will still need to think about the stories, product, images and so on that will grab their attention.

Even if you are not going to have your own store, you will need to find a way to educate the retail managers and sales assistants in the stores to which you will wholesale. For many of your customers these third-party representatives will be their first contact with your brand. The more they know about the product and your philosophy, the easier it will be for them to sell your line.

Sales manager:
* Manages new and existing accounts
* Builds relationships
* Sets sales targets
* Inputs orders and deals with customer deliveries and returns
* Maintains the showroom and books in sales appointments
* Selects which exhibitions and promotional fashion shows to take part in
* Is responsible for the distribution of samples, price lists and lookbooks.

Allocator:
* Distributes orders to stores, making sure the correct sizes and volumes reach the right stores
* Chases suppliers for production
* Oversees stock replenishment and reorders.

PR/Marketing manager:
* Promotes the brand and its products, using advertising, public relations, sales promotion, personal selling, visual merchandising and the internet
* Develops and maintains media relations across fashion stylists, journalists and editors
* Plans and executes company events from fashion shows to photo shoots and press days.

Fashion stylist:
* Creates visual looks for catwalk shows and images, such as photographs used in lookbooks, ad campaigns, websites and fashion editorials.

Stylists play an important role in getting the overall visual presentation of a collection right, whether it be for a catwalk show, lookbook or advertising campaign

Fashion journalist:

* Analyses and/or promotes fashion products
* Communicates the constantly changing fashion market to the consumer.

Retail manager:

* Is responsible for the day-to-day running of a store or department, maximising sales and profit
* Manages and motivates a team to increase sales and ensure efficiency.

Sales assistant:

* The 'face' of the shop, responsible for promoting and selling products direct to customers
* Liaises with clients (in all areas, client interaction is vital and sales assistants working with higher-priced goods will need to take a very personalised approach).

The key to the success of a one-person operation is to focus on the area you do well in and know when to outsource to trained professionals. Obviously, the more roles you are able to deliver yourself the fewer costs you will incur; however, don't spread yourself too thin. In the long run a little expenditure on staff in the right places can go a very long way.

===

TASKS

1   Identify how many of these roles you will undertake yourself. Make a list of those you will need to outsource.

2   Research local fashion colleges for potential talent and read ads in fashion trade magazines to get an idea of salaries and freelance wages in your area.

===

Hiring and Firing

Being the boss means that you are responsible for appointing the right personnel, managing your team and firing ineffective staff. Without any managerial experience this can often be a daunting task. Although you may be in a rush with the workload starting to pile up, make sure you take your time finding the right candidates. The worst thing for any small fashion label is to recruit someone who doesn't live up to your expectations. The interview process is your opportunity to make sure you are getting the right person for the job.

Tips for Interviewers

===

Charlotte Kramer *– Human Resources Specialist and Executive*

THE FOUR P's

Preparation
In advance of the interview, review the candidate's curriculum vitae and prepare a list of relevant questions.

Professionalism
You are a representative of your organisation, so be prompt to the meeting and professional throughout. Furthermore, consider that whilst you are deciding whether to hire the candidate, the candidate will be contemplating whether he or she would like to work for you. At the end of the interview process, follow up to let the candidate know the outcome.

Productive
Begin the meeting with a brief outline of the interview process, provide an overview of the organisation and the mission. Outline the role, including key responsibilities, objectives and any team structure. Pose a series of pertinent questions and subsequently encourage the candidate to put questions to you.

Probing
Make certain interview questions favour the 'open' technique: 'Tell me about a time when you...' and 'Give me an example of...'. Explore past performance, skills and qualifications. Seek to understand potential weaknesses and areas for greater development: 'Tell me about an aspect of your role you wish to improve.'

===

Keep Them Motivated

Once you have the right people you need to keep them motivated. As a start-up fashion business you can't afford to have anyone on the team who is content just to pick up a pay packet. You need your team to be ambitious and as hungry as you are for the business to establish itself. Try to create an environment that means your staff can flourish. This means you need to:

- ✖ **Pay attention:** It is all too easy to become bogged down in your own day-to-day activities. Be aware of how your staff are feeling and acting.

- ✖ **Implement an appraisal scheme:** Everybody wants feedback on how they are performing. By setting a schedule for constructive feedback you will also have a platform for discussing how you feel your staff are doing. In the first year a one-month, three-month, six-month and twelve-month review are advisable, with an annual appraisal after that.

- ✖ **Offer training and development:** Consider offering further training for staff members to fill any skills gaps or to increase their knowledge base.

- ✖ **Create a collaborative and friendly work culture:** In a small, creative business it is important to create the right atmosphere. Whilst some people flourish in a dictatorial environment, people usually need some room to express themselves. Your success will be determined by how productive your staff are and how long they stay working for you. As a start-up fashion label you can't afford a high staff turnover.

Sometimes you will have to let people go. Firing someone can be a horrible experience and can become even worse if you find yourself being sued for unfair dismissal. You must make sure you follow the correct steps when terminating someone's employment.

Things to Think About When Considering Terminating the Employment of an Employee

===

Charlotte Kramer – Human Resources Specialist and Executive

- -

- ✖ *Maintain documentation demonstrating examples of under-performance/conduct as well as written records of performance discussions and developmental plans.*
- ✖ *Address all possible areas for improvement, such as participation in relevant training and development courses or an appropriate behavioural programme.*
- ✖ *Adhere to disciplinary policies/local employment legislation.*
- ✖ *Consider suitable alternative employment opportunities within the organisation.*
- ✖ *Treat the employee fairly.*
- ✖ *Act with sensitivity and confidentiality.*

===

Case Study: Gil Carvalho

In the autumn of 2003, at the age of 27, Portuguese footwear designer Gil Carvalho set up Carvalho Concept Ltd, a high-end luxury ladies' shoe label. He had studied at Cordwainers College, part of the London College of Fashion, graduating with a first class BA in Design, Marketing and Product Development, and then went on to work for Vivienne Westwood.

After a brief stint with Westwood, Gil realised that his future lay in the formation of his own company. 'The decision to launch my own company was so that I could have total control over my product from concept to production.' With the help of some close friends he set about developing his first ready-to-wear collection, along with a conceptual collection to help him reach his ultimate goal – to have the name Gil Carvalho synonymous with luxury.

The first season's collection was entirely self-financed and included a total of 12 styles, each in three colour options. Prices ranged from £190 to £1,000. Gil has had a lot of success since he started the label, but it took three years for the company to break even.

Gil believes that patience is important when running a fashion business. He also sees drive and perseverance as two major reasons for his success. He says that 'it helps to know your own mind, because everybody involved in fashion has an opinion!'

Understanding his target market was a key factor for Gil in both his sales and manufacturing strategy. 'Luxury ladies' shoes are synonymous with Italian production so I felt there was really no choice but to manufacture there.' He then decided to target the UK market, but soon became aware of the international appeal of the shoes and started to pursue the US and Italian markets.

Wholesale is an important part of Gil's sales strategy and, although he plans at some stage to open his own retail premises, at this stage he recognises that it is too early to be considering the expense of a shop. As he is looking to attract an international market he has taken his product to a number of trade shows and, after initial research, narrowed it down to Micam in Milan, WSA in Las Vegas and Première Classe in Paris. There were more, but these were consider...

important and met his strict budget demands at the beginning. As the company expands he is looking at involvement in other shows, and his export business now accounts for the largest part of his overall sales.

Gil sees promotion as a key part of the success of a fashion business, placing it ahead of placement and price. 'Never underestimate the effects of good PR; in fashion this is extremely important and cannot be underestimated. PR is fundamental; get this right and the rest follows.' However Gil believes that one of the biggest challenges to getting good PR is 'market saturation and getting the industry to take notice. All too often the magazines, the main point of reference for the customer, stick to the established brands and give scant regard to new and emerging talent.'

In an attempt to break into the established media Gil initially looked to outsource his PR to an agency but very soon decided that the best way forward was to establish his own in-house PR. This allowed him to reduce his outgoings and make sure that the product remained his priority. He has also decided to look at the catwalk as a means of promoting his label but admits it can be difficult as shoes 'are seen as the accessory to the main event, which is an obstacle that must be overcome'. He believes that product visibility is of the utmost importance and that the catwalk is often one of the best ways to achieve this, allowing you to 'showcase a more extreme and conceptual product, which draws attention to your work'.

One of the biggest motivations for Gil is 'seeing my shoes on the shelves and feeding the shoe-lover's addiction with a must-have design! On a more serious note, the opportunities that present themselves once people begin to appreciate your work are massively important. For me, the recognition of someone established in the industry, ... ose work I love, is the ultimate accolade.'

In order to receive an international audience, Gil wholesales his shoes through trade shows in London, Las Vegas, Paris and Milan

*F*ar too many new fashion labels spend the first three to four seasons finding out who their customers are, where they shop and what is and isn't right for them. The more you know about the market you are about to enter, the more you can be sure about the viability of your product. More importantly, the more research you undertake before you start to put money down on developing your first sample range, the more money you will save in the long run. This chapter will take you through the market research process.

Research Your Market

Market research is all about obtaining and analysing information in order to make sure you have the right product to deliver to your customer. It also plays a major role in supporting your business plan. Investors or banks will want to know what research you have undertaken to back up your projections. This can be achieved through 'secondary' research (information in the press, databases, directories, reports and books) as well as your own 'primary' research (original information obtained through surveys and observation). The latter will be more focused and therefore more useful.

Know Your Customer

You need to know who your customers are. Many young designers develop products at a price point that they themselves could not afford. They often make assumptions about customers and their buying habits. You need to know everything about the types of people who will buy your product if you are to develop a product that meets their needs and wants.

You need to find out about your customers' spending habits, lifestyle, likes and dislikes and, most importantly, their needs. Knowing why people are buying your product makes it easier to give them the ideal product. Spending time in boutiques and stores, watching how customers shop and what product they pick up and buy can be a great way of getting to know your customer. Working in a retail establishment that you hope to sell to can be invaluable. If you have direct access to people's buying habits and seasonal expenditure you can start to develop your product around this. You will begin to get an idea of what they feel is missing from their wardrobe. Failing this, getting out on the street in a shopping district where your competitors are located and asking passers-by specific questions can give you a pretty good understanding of their buying habits, needs and wants, and how best to grab their attention.

Fashion hall at Bread & Butter trade show, Barcelona

Profiling Your Target Customer

Demographic	Buying Habits	Likes/Dislikes
Occupation?	Where do they shop?	Favourite designer?
Age?	How do they shop (impulse, sales, seasonally)?	What magazines do they read?
Married, single, divorced?	Are they trend-driven?	What newspaper do they read?
Do they have children?	Are they brand-loyal?	What celebrity do they admire?
Annual income?	What function do they buy for (casual or occasion)?	What is their biggest dislike in fashion?
Where do they live?	How body-conscious are they (enhance or hide)?	What makes them laugh?
Where do they go on holiday?	What is their spending bracket?	What music do they listen to?
How many holidays do they take a year?		
What size do they wear?		

TASK

Create a customer profile
Answer the above questions to create a profile of your ideal customer. Try to create as many different profiles as possible, so that when you market and promote your brand or shop you cover all possible angles. Ask yourself any other questions that you feel might help you better understand your customer.

Having identified your ideal customer, you need to be certain there are enough of them for you to supply. Looking at other fashion labels that offer similar products to yours can give you an indication of this.

Watch Your Competitors

Studying your potential competitors will save you a lot of time and money by using research that others have already undertaken. If similar offers on the market are doing well you can feel confident that a market exists for your product line. First, however, you must decide exactly who your market rivals will be.

By identifying similar labels you can target their current stockist list, knowing that your product will be appreciated. You can also see exactly the types of style, colourway, length, print, trim and so on that work well for your competitors. Most importantly, you will be able to identify what your customer will expect to pay for certain products, at entry, mid and top-end price points. If you identify the wrong competitors at the beginning you will waste a lot of time and energy targeting the wrong retailers and customer base. Take your time and get it right.

It is unrealistic to expect retailers and customers to see you in the same light as a superbrand such as Gucci or Ralph Lauren without the history and brand recognition behind you. There are many fashion labels that you may never have heard of but that are doing very good business. A number of your direct competitors probably already exist within this group and you will be able to

Attending trade shows is a great way of researching your competition

gather a lot more information about their activities than about those of any of the big established labels.

Going to trade fairs, identifying similar labels, seeing where they stock (not only shops but countries) and looking at the PR they have achieved will help you to build a business template and develop a better understanding of who will buy your product and why.

Just because you see a label in major fashion publications doesn't mean it is thriving. The fashion industry has a history of PR-friendly labels that have littered the pages of *Vogue*, *Harper's Bazaar* and *Elle* and are now never heard of. Make sure you do your research properly, identifying labels that have both commercial and press appeal.

===

TASK

Analyse the competition
Choose one competitor already selling in your market and do a SWOT analysis of them (see page 100). Can you exploit any of their weaknesses or threats?

===

Tailor Your Product to Your Market

What will make your product special (see Chapter 9)? Start by identifying your competitors' strengths and weaknesses and see how you can beat their offer.

You need to identify what is already on the market – otherwise you cannot guarantee that you won't just be offering more of the same, but worse, at a higher price. The fashion business is very unforgiving – having the wrong product or price will lead to rejection of your label. Work out how you should tailor your product to meet your customers' needs and how this will give you an edge.

The fashion market is very crowded, with thousands of labels competing worldwide for distribution. You need to have a USP to break into the market and create a viable business. The more time you spend looking at labels that have been on the market for some time, or new ones that are making a splash, the easier it will be for you to determine what it is that makes them successful.

Get the Price Right
The success of your label will also depend on correct pricing for your market. Having studied your competitors' product lines you should have been able to identify a pricing structure. What are their entry (cheapest), mid-range and high-end (most expensive) price points and how much of each item do they offer at

Womenswear label Noir has successfully tailored its product to fit into a new and expanding market aimed at combining ethical fashion with designer luxury (see page 18)

each end of the pricing spectrum (see Chapter 9)? You should also be able to get an understanding of the detailing, finish and design required to sell the product at that price point. If your competitor is selling a printed silk top for £135 and the product is similar to your product, you can establish that there is a market at that price point for your offer. Just double check that your competitor actually has a successful business. If you log on to their website and find they are stocking in a number of stores, they are probably doing well.

Most customers will have a limit on how much they will pay for a particular product. A designer dress selling at up to £295 may be within their limit, but as soon as you hit the £300 mark a barrier will come down. Luxury shoppers, however, might feel £300 is too inexpensive – the dress is not exclusive enough. By offering the right product at the right price you will promote both customer loyalty and referral and move your fashion label a step closer to becoming a viable business.

===

TASK

Identify a competitor's pricing structure
Analyse the pricing structure of one of your competitors. Identify entry, mid and high-end price points, then make a list of each style on offer and their retail price. How many pieces are there at entry to mid price points and how many at mid to high-end?

===

Marketing and PR

Marketing and PR will be very important in the development and overall success of your label (see Chapter 12). You need to know which media your potential customer taps into. This includes the newspapers, magazines and websites they look to for information, as well as the best places to grab their attention with any proposed advertising. Without this insight your advertising and promotional campaigns will be a stab in the dark. Although every designer may want their product to appear in *Vogue,* appearing in *Elle* may do more for your business in reaching your target consumer and turning good PR and advertising into actual sales. If this is the case you should concentrate more of your efforts on developing relationships with the staff at *Elle.* Equally, you may spend a lot of time and energy organising a catwalk show to promote your label when the money might be better spent on trade exhibitions and press days.

Determine from the outset which media you need to target. You need to know the publications your target customer reads to make sure you are targeting the right one. You can phone the advertising desk of any publication to find out the demographic of their readership. They have this information on hand for potential advertisers who want to make sure they are targeting the right consumer.

Channels of Distribution

How your customer has access to your product will determine how they will view your brand and its image.

Is your business is going to be retail, wholesale or both? Whatever you decide will have a major impact on the financing of your business and on your marketing and PR strategy. Researching how some of your competitors started up and developed their business can be a good starting point for determining your distribution strategy. Websites often give details of a company's history and growth.

You can, once again, look to your competition for an indication of the best outlets for your product. If you are wholesaling, you will want to find out at which exhibitions and showrooms your competitors showcase their collections. National fashion councils and exhibition websites will provide this information. You can also look at your competitors' websites for their lists of current stockists – if a shop has bought their product it may be interested in yours.

Where and how your product is introduced to the consumer is of great importance

If you want to open a retail outlet you may find that by looking your competitors in the eye (setting up your store in the same street or area) you are able to piggyback on their marketing activities and build a customer base from existing passing shoppers. Just make sure that the competition isn't too fierce and the potential share of customers too small.

===

TASK

Develop a list of potential stockists
Visit stores that you would like to sell to, and identify ten competitors whose product you would like to see yours sitting next to. Visit their websites to view their lists of current stockists. Research the stockists to establish what other brands they sell and then visit the websites of these brands to see if their product complements yours. If it does, look at their stockist lists and continue cross-referencing stockists with brands until you have a sizeable database that you can use for the PR and marketing of your first collection.

===

Find the Right Location

Location is absolutely fundamental to success if you aim to retail. Spend time deciding where will be the best location for you to set up to maximise your potential to sell: high street, shopping centre/mall, freestanding, website, markets or home shopping parties (see Chapter 11).

Getting the right location for your retail store is vital

Retail Checklist

Demographic
Is the area mainly residential or business? Are income levels in this area generally high or low? What is the average shopper like?

Market trend information
How progressive is the community? Does it promote business activity? Is it receptive to change? Are shops open in the evenings or on Sundays? How many businesses opened and closed during the last 12 months? What are the major employers in the community? What is the anticipated growth in the area around the potential site? What are the business trends of the community?

Competition information
Using a map, place an 'X' where the competitors are located. Circle the best potential sites. Complete an analysis of each competitor. Are your competitors currently involved in any advertising or promotional activities?

Traffic and accessibility
✖ *Distance from residential areas*	✖ *Public transport*
✖ *Distance from business areas*	✖ *Best side of the street*
✖ *Parking availability*	✖ *Location on street*
✖ *Traffic congestion*	✖ *Appropriate business neighbours*

When does a normal shopping situation occur?
✖ *Day of the week*	✖ *Season*
✖ *Time of day*	✖ *Weather conditions*
✖ *Week of the month*	

Cost considerations
✖ *Rent/mortgage*	✖ *Decorating*
✖ *Business rates*	✖ *Security*
✖ *Utilities*	✖ *Insurance*
✖ *Improvements*	✖ *Other*

Terms of the lease
✖ *Length of lease*	✖ *Option to renew*
✖ *Option to purchase*	✖ *Amount of rent and when payable*
✖ *Description of the space*	✖ *Restrictions on remodelling*
✖ *Restrictions on posting of signs*	✖ *Landlord's responsibilities*
✖ *Insurance requirements*	✖ *Status of tenant if space is sold*
✖ *Sub-letting arrangements*	

Anne Fontaine established her Anne Fontaine womenswear label in Paris in 1993 at the age of 22. Often referred to as 'the Queen of the White Shirt', she has seen her business grow rapidly over the past 15 years from her first boutique in Paris in 1994 into an internationally renowned global empire with stores represented in major cities, including New York's Madison Avenue (opened 2000), Shanghai (opened 2005) and Tokyo (opened 2006).

From the very outset Anne and her husband and business partner Ari Zlotkin focused their business around the core concepts of 'simplicity, innovation and independence', and have worked to offer a female customer base 'a grand vision of contemporary luxury' that still remains at the heart of their business today. By 2004, sales had risen to €70 million, they employed almost 400 staff and their product was sold at 65 points of sale in 14 countries worldwide.

Though not having formally studied fashion, Anne's creativity was evident at an early age when she made her own clothes. A journey through the heart of the Amazonian rainforest instilled in her a love for natural materials and their virtues, and would serve as the basis for the Anne Fontaine brand. It was, however, the chance discovery of an old white shirt that would find Anne imagining 'a place where any woman could find such a simple shirt, or blouse, or cache-coeur (crossover top) – the basics of a wardrobe – that would permit her to choose a fashion point of view according to her mood' and serve as the catalyst for the start of the business.

Anne approached Ari with the idea of designing the very first collection of white shirts entirely for women. Over 500 styles were conceived in that first season from her initial concept, which were then whittled down into a smaller selection to launch the very first Anne Fontaine collection. Anne's experience in the rainforest and her natural sensitivities towards environmental issues had exposed her to the vast array of natural fibres and allowed her to explore within such a simple concept as 'the white shirt' a multitude of options to offer her clients.

What started with poplin, piqué cotton and organdie soon included linen, lace and many other new season. 'The fabrics serve as a source of inspiration not only through their intrinsic form, but also through the particular qualities that temper their feeling upon contact with the skin.'

After the choice of fabrics came the development of signature details within her designs: double collars, embroidered flowers, lacing, or vertiges, a word that Anne employs to refer to 'highly personal ruching which appears in a variety of different forms in each collection.' Ultimately, Anne is looking to offer her customers 'allure' and believes this has been the key to her success. With the right cut and a mastery of fabrics she has been able to offer the wearer 'a second skin, a familiar and reliable piece of clothing that guarantees a natural and spontaneous elegance that can stem only from the natural sense of breathability that it gives to the woman wearing it.'

Comfort and functionality also play a huge part in the objective of Anne's designs and every season she looks for 'new approaches to elegance adapted to every personality and every possible mix of occasions.' And while new ideas are constantly being developed the process remains the same as when she first started, with 500 new designs being put forward for consideration twice a year. 'It's still the very same struggle to decide just which ones will make up the 100 select models to be set out for American, Japanese, Chinese or French customers in the shops of Paris, New York or Tokyo.'

Product and vision remain at the heart of the Anne Fontaine brand, but the virtues of the materials that Anne sees as so essential to the success of her clothing range are not limited to clothing alone and, taking inspiration from her Amazonian experiences, she has developed the Anne Fontaine Spa, where she is able to share her experience of 'the therapeutic virtues of these natural treasures. Cotton, silk and wild bamboo are at the heart of the signature treatments at Spa Anne Fontaine, and lay the grounds for its exclusivity.'

Twelve years after opening the first Anne Fontaine Boutique in Paris, the new location on Rue Saint-Honoré was opened in 2006, allowing Anne, for the first time, to present her complete vision for the brand by uniting a boutique and spa.

The Anne Fontaine boutique on Rue Saint-Honoré, Paris, was opened in 2006. The boutique allows Anne for the first time to deliver her complete concept for the brand with the Anne Fontaine Spa sitting next to her trademark white shirts under one roof

Chapter 8: Understanding Trends

*T*rends play an important role in the world of fashion; you must understand how they work and how you can use them to your best advantage. You will have to decide how focused on trends your particular customer base is. Your initial research should have given you a good understanding of your potential customer and you should be able to determine whether your shopper is trend-driven. You should develop your product accordingly. Your product success will be determined by your ability to meet the needs of your customers. This chapter will show you how to find out what your customers actually want and how they are influenced by trends.

What Is a Fashion Trend?

A 'fashion trend' can be defined as the movement of fashion over a period of time. What is in fashion one season may be out the next. Fashion trends are all about the 'latest' or the 'newest'. In recent years, 'new' has tended to mean that the product has been missing or scarce in the marketplace for a while and is being reintroduced by designers or retailers. It may only be truly new to the generation of consumers who missed the trend the first time around.

Trends do not have to be seasonal. The 1990s saw the start of a trend for more casual dressing in the workplace that still can be seen today.

Other trends burst into the stores, are worn for a very limited time, then disappear just as quickly as they emerged. These varying lifespans of trends are known as 'fashion cycles'. A trend's fashion cycle is determined by the number of people (adopters) that buy into the look and how quickly it takes for the look to take off and eventually die out. In order for something to become fashionable it has to be accepted by the consumer. Although a designer or retailer may push a particular style, if it is not bought and worn there is no trend.

Different Categories of Trend
Within the fashion cycle itself we can identify different categories of trends by looking at the lifespan of the trend as well as the speed of the rise and decline of the adoption period. Some of the key differences within the cycle include:

Classics
A fashion look that has been around longer than expected. Retailers sell classics season after season. Examples include the white shirt, the trench coat and the little black dress (LBD). The style never completely dies.

Tokyo street style

Fads

Fads are those products that have a very short shelf-life, arriving on the scene with a big splash, only to disappear just as quickly. Although fads have a short lifecycle, savvy designers and retailers are able to capitalise on fads to keep customers and the press interested.

Cycles within cycles

Successful designers are able to tinker with design elements (such as colour, texture or silhouette) to offer 'newness' to a popular product, keeping it fresh and maximising its lifespan. A great example of this is, again, the LBD, which has become a staple of any fashionista's wardrobe. It is always being updated.

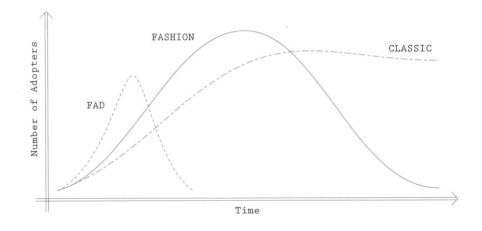

Fashions are classified as a classic or a fad by looking at how quickly they progress through the six phases of the fashion lifecycle. A fad may go through all six stages within one season, whereas a classic may never reach stage six, declining only for a while before being reintroduced.

Fashion Lifecycle Phases

===

1 **Innovation:** *Fashion leaders will pay high prices for new looks.*
2 **Rise:** *More people start to adopt the key looks.*
3 **Acceleration:** *The look is copied by many retailers and adopted by fashion followers.*
4 **General acceptance:** *The look reaches its maximum sales potential and is to be seen everywhere.*
5 **Decline:** *Sales decline as new trends emerge; retailers reduce prices and start to replace the look with a newer trend.*
6 **Obsolescence:** *The look is no longer to be seen.*

===

Who Leads and Who Follows Fashion

It is the fashion leaders who drive new looks forward, but a trend truly relies on the fashion followers to legitimise it.

Diffusion of Innovation

In 1962 Everett Rogers formulated his 'diffusion of innovations' theory in his book, *Diffusion of Innovations*. He argued that adopters of any new innovation or idea could be categorised as innovators (2.5%), early adopters (13.5%), early majority (34%), late majority (34%) and laggards (16%). He argued that the willingness and ability of each group to adopt an innovation would depend on their awareness, interest, evaluation and trial. Although this theory can sometimes be over-simplistic, it goes a long way towards defining the key attributes and reasons behind trend adoption. Here are some of the key characteristics defining each group:

Fashion innovators

These are the earliest communicators of a new style or look to other fashion consumers. They may or may not be influential in making other people like the style, but they create the awareness and provide the visual display and initial exposure of the style. They feel more socially secure and are more interested in fashion than others.

Early adopters

Early adopters legitimise a style for fashion followers. They influence people in their social group but stay within the social norms of the group. They may also adopt a slightly modified or toned-down version of a style after innovators have received attention from others. Early adopters are crucial for the mainstreaming of trends.

Early majority

The early majority are very deliberate in their purchases and look to those more stylish for guidance. They are influenced by advertising and media but are more driven to look good for the sake of fitting in with those around them.

Late majority

The late majority are more sceptical of the 'latest' or 'newest' fashions and will take time to be convinced. However, they want to be considered part of the group and will therefore follow the herd. They tend to have more traditional tastes and quite often come from lower socio-economic backgrounds.

Laggards

Laggards look to neighbours and friends. They are looking for comfort and ease of wear and are not interested in trends. They also have a fear of debt and are therefore the least likely to impulse-buy.

We tend to define those in the first two groups as 'change agents' or 'innovative communicators' – those people that help to move fashion forward. Those in the remaining groups are 'fashion followers', and tend to look to others for guidelines.

When plotted on a graph, Rogers' theory of diffusion looks like this:

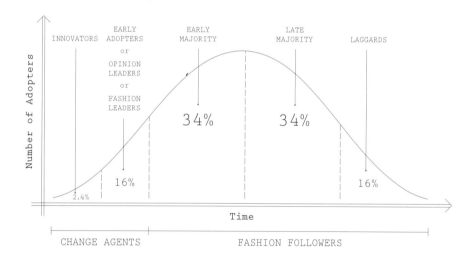

A market exists at each of these stages, with the consumers in the biggest market segments being considered fashion followers. You will therefore need to decide in which segment your ideal customer sits and develop your product line accordingly.

Rogers also proposed a five-stage model for the diffusion of innovation. He argued that adopters would go through each stage before ultimately deciding whether or not to accept the innovation.

1   **Knowledge:** Learning about the existence and function of the innovation.

2   **Persuasion:** Becoming convinced of the value of the innovation.

3   **Decision:** Committing to the adoption of the innovation.

4   *Implementation:* Putting the innovation to use.

5   *Confirmation:* The ultimate acceptance (or rejection) of the innovation.

If you consider yourself an innovative designer and are hoping to develop new trends, your marketing and PR will have to work hard to get the customer to work through these five stages. Many great young designers don't even get enough exposure to let the consumer know their product exists, let alone give them the chance to buy it and offer confirmation of the look. The catwalk is usually the place for this type of design and you will need to target the fashion press to gain the initial recognition you will require.

Characteristics of Innovators v Early Adopters/Mainstream

Innovators	Early Adopter/Mainstream
Creative	Want entertainment, to consume
Participators	Spectators; just read about it
Risk-takers	Want comfort, to fit in
Create own identity	Ease of mass market and media definition
Unusual level of passion	Want safety, to fit in, to go where the herd goes
Interested in change/novelty	Like comfort and stability, don't think too much

High Fashion v Mass Fashion

✖ *High-fashion looks are created by designers and exclusive stores.*
✖ *Fashion leaders buy these looks during the introduction and growth stages.*
✖ *The goods are expensive but exclusivity is what fashion leaders crave.*

✖ *Mass fashion is made by manufacturers and retailers at many price points.*
✖ *Fashion followers wear mass fashion.*
✖ *Fashion laggards want good value; they buy late.*

What Influences Fashion Trends?

Several factors influence fashion trends from season to season and from decade to decade. These can include: technology, economic conditions, social conditions, media, celebrities and peer groups.

Designers are influenced by their surroundings and current events. Moods and feelings play an important part in the development of designs and different

designers are often influenced by the same factors – this can be seen in their designs. In times of uncertainty it is common to see more structure and tailoring in muted colours on the catwalks. When things begin to pick up you may see vibrant colours combined with fluid tailoring and fabrics.

Trends may develop along a safe and predictable route – from a previous season's product or as a reaction against a trend that has become saturated. Designers and retailers can also be cautious about introducing a trend. They may introduce some product into their stores to test their customers' reactions before putting their money into a big production run. This is known as a 'trial balloon'. If the product is not well received it will disappear from the store and not become a trend.

Before committing large amounts of their budget, retailers will often see how customers react to a new trend by trialling the product in-store

Theories of Fashion Leadership

Several theories have been developed about how fashion spreads:

'Trickle down' theory

Fashion spreads from the top down. At the top are the fashion icons and style gurus. The high street and the consumer watch what is happening on the catwalks or being worn by the celebrities and interpret the trends to fit into their market or lifestyle.

Royal figures (Diana, Princess of Wales) and celebrities (David Beckham, Paris Hilton) can become fashion icons, legitimising a look for the general public and having a huge influence on sales. This is one of the reasons why so many designers try so hard to get their product on an A-lister's back. A single picture of the right celebrity can be syndicated worldwide, giving your product and label instant global exposure (see Chapter 12).

'Trickle across' theory

Fashion spreads horizontally within and across groups. Each segment of society will have its own leaders to whom it will look for guidance on what is and isn't acceptable. This can range from a young executive looking to the boss for behavioural and dress guidelines, to a group of friends, of whom one is a trendsetter. Most of us want to fit in, so we won't be the first to adopt a new look and will require affirmation of the trend from others around us. However, we don't want to be the last to adopt the look as we will then look out of place. Ultimately, our need to fit in dictates our adoption of certain trends.

'Trickle up' theory

Trends that have their origins within sub-groups of society will often find their way upwards into the mainstream. Both the high-street stores and high-end designers will often look to street culture for their inspiration. Think of how the fashions of US hip hop culture have gone mainstream in retailers all over the world, and have even found their way on to the catwalks of London, Paris, New York and Milan.

Trends may trickle down, across and up to reach their target customer. The more tuned in you are to what is taking place on the catwalks, on the streets and among your own friends, the easier it will be to identify potential trends. Many designers don't go out of their way to predict a trend, but their ongoing search for inspiration often means they are on-trend season after season.

Media Influences on Trends

The media plays a very important role in influencing what is and isn't on-trend. Designers and retailers create themes within a seasonal collection, with a selection of looks that will appeal to as broad a range of buyers as possible. Themes across different designer collections tend to happen because designers and fabric manufacturers have to predict so far ahead that they work to a creative formula. By studying previous trends and the current mood and environment designers can predict, albeit often subconsciously, where the market is progressing or even returning to.

Fashion writers, who see hundreds of fashion shows and lookbooks each season, will group the work of the designers in order to write about it in a way their reader can understand. This means looking at key pieces and themes that stick out in enough of the collections to get their attention. Buyers from boutiques and department stores also take note of the trends and work out which will appeal to their customers. Customers read about what's hot and what's not – when the new looks and trends appear in the fashion press a demand is created, and the boutiques and department stores are then ready to sell the garments that have been praised and singled out.

How Trend-Driven Should You Be?

This depends on the customer you aim to target. You may decide that being a slave to the trends would actually be detrimental to your business, and focus more on developing a uniqueness of your own that your customer will want season after season (see Chapter 9).

It is difficult to compete with the bigger labels and high-street stores in the trend stakes. High-street stores will have a number of different trends each season, safe in the knowledge that if one doesn't take off as well as they hoped they have others the consumer can buy into. If you have put all your eggs in one basket and then discover that the look for the season isn't the one you decided on, the effect on your sales will be devastating.

However, cleverly introducing elements of trends into your collection – colour, fabric, sizing and styling – whilst not taking away the essence of who and what your label is, can help to move your product forward. Being on-trend can also help in attracting the attention of fashion magazines that need to show their readers the latest looks.

You could try to allocate a percentage of your collection each season to experiment with trend-led ideas. This will give you the freedom to create new

When developing a collection, designers will often introduce elements of trend relevant to each season (waistcoat, oversized shirt, skinny trousers) whilst still offering their more classic pieces (wrap dress)

and exciting ideas whilst focusing the rest of the collection on your already established, tried-and-tested designs.

You may also find that, depending on where your customer sits in the diffusion of innovation (see page 84), that being off-trend is more beneficial to your sales. This is because mainstreamers won't necessarily buy into a new trend straight away and may take another season or two to feel confident that it is right for them. Even when they do buy into the look it is usually a watered-down version. It is therefore imperative to understand the expectations of your customer and develop your product accordingly.

High-end designers are often instrumental in setting the trends for the upcoming seasons, and if this is where you hope your label will sit then you will need to be true to your own vision rather than following others. You will need to work hard at convincing both the press and consumers that your vision is worth their attention. Once you have achieved this you will find that you are being watched for tips for next season. Until this happens, you may be developing innovative designs that nobody wants to wear.

Decide from the start where you believe your customer sits in the trend stakes and look at your competitors to see how trend-driven they really are. You may find that both place more importance on good, well thought-out design.

===

TASK

Walk through your local shopping district and look at the window displays. Look for any themes running through the product on show. Don't forget to look at colour, fabric and style of accessories as well as garments.

===

Case Study: Schumacher

In 1989, 24-year-old Dorothee Schumacher established Schumacher in Germany. The label, which started off with five special pieces, has grown into an internationally recognisable brand synonymous with high-quality, sophisticated, yet contemporary pieces for women. Prices range from €69 for a basic shirt, to €399 for dresses and up to €1,200 for a key collection piece. Dorothee's aim was always to place Schumacher in the most beautiful shop windows internationally, in stores located next to names such as Chanel and Hermès and, almost 20 years on, this still is the essence of the Schumacher sales strategy. The label began by presenting its key pieces at the Collection Première Düsseldorf, one of the world's most important fashion fairs. After initial success in Germany, interest in the label grew in Switzerland and Austria, almost immediately followed by global success. Schumacher has remained a family-run business.

From a very early age Dorothee knew what she wanted to achieve. Fascinated by the flair that surrounds the fashion industry, she went to Italy and France to study textiles. She worked with a number of well-known brands, constantly watching, learning and developing her own unique style that would serve as the building blocks for the launch of her own label.

From the beginning the product has always come first for Dorothee, who started by designing a shirt that 'was different from any other – smart, feminine and powerful.' Dorothee believes 'the Schumacher woman relies on her feminine charm as opposed to emulating the male way of dressing', and that it has been this understanding of her customers' needs, combined with her own sense of creativity, that led to the immediate success of her first and subsequent collections. Dorothee feels that it is important for any new label to have 'a very strong sense of style and intuitive feel for forthcoming trends, confidence and conviction, not to mention the perfect balance between the customer's needs and not compromising one's own ideas.' Having started with only five pieces, the Schumacher collection now offers a complete range, including coats, dresses, knitwear, T-shirts and accessories.

To ensure that the large product range stands up to the scrutiny that Dorothee herself places on each piece, huge importance is placed on the manufacturing process and where the product is made: 'In the early years, manufacturing was done exclusively in Italy and Germany, but by 1996–97 Schumacher began to identify countries with the highest level of knowhow in specific fields – embroidery in India, cashmere in Italy and lace in France – thus guaranteeing the highest quality at all times.' This ensures that 'the product remains at the heart of our strategy and symbolises the philosophy and authenticity of Schumacher.' It also means that 'because of all the love and hard work, the Schumacher product competes with other luxury products in the high-price segment.'

While getting the price right is obviously an important factor in the development of a label, Dorothee says it is not the most important one. 'When a customer finds "the piece", they are always willing to pay for it', and, as a result, she ranks price behind product and placement. The promotion of the label is developed through an extensive marketing strategy that focuses on the heart of the Schumacher brand. 'All our packages, give-aways and shop essentials are unique. The customer does not just buy a piece, but a complete look and the philosophy surrounding it. Everything is made with love and dedication. Schumacher works on word-of-mouth recommendation, therefore our policy is strictly against advertising and licensing.' They maintain their PR department in-house at their headquarters but work closely with external agencies for international PR.

While Dorothee recognises there can be disappointments when running your own fashion label she says that 'one needs to be positive and always look forward'. Her constant motivation comes from 'the people surrounding me; the permanent change and regeneration of Schumacher and everything it stands for. I am always eager to learn and having my own brand gives me the opportunity to do this on a day-to-day basis. It is exciting to grow and to enter new arenas. I thrive on new experiences and meeting great people.' She views Schumacher as a great platform for all her creative thoughts that allows her to be a businesswoman. It also allows her to structure her life the way she wants. 'By being able to bring my dreams to life I gain a lot of strength. Schumacher also gives me the opportunity to organise my time the way it is best for me and my family.'

From an initial collection of just five pieces, Dorothee Schumacher has grown her label into an international brand that she operates from her headquarters in Germany

*D*eveloping your own product is your chance to
express yourself creatively and produce something you
feel good about – probably the reason you started on this
journey. But it is even more important to ensure that you
have a strong profile and a good customer rating. This
chapter will outline the rules for making sure that the line
you develop creates the impact you need.

Understand Your Customer

If you are serious about developing a clothing line that will allow you to create
a lasting business, you must do your market research and have a full
understanding of your target customer's lifestyle. Without an understanding of
your customer base it is very difficult to determine not only what they will wear
but on what occasion they will wear it.

Small start-up fashion labels can often be self-indulgent, designing with
themselves in mind, in the blind self-belief that 'I just know other people will
love it!' Although this can be good if your taste reflects that of the markets and
you fit the profile of your target customer, it is usually a fast-track to failure.

Many young designers starting out do not have the lifestyle, let alone the bank
balance, of their target customer and are not designer shoppers themselves.
This means that they often make assumptions about the people they hope to
sell to, and their product often fails to meet the needs of the consumer.

You need to identify your competitors, analyse what does and doesn't sell for
them, determine what your prospective customer is likely to buy and refine
your product range accordingly (see Chapter 7).

Getting It Right

If you are going to make your mark, you need to cover all the angles.

Direction and Mood

'Direction' and 'mood' are the intangible design elements that are often the
difference between success and failure. If you can create a collection that has
an immediate message and attitude, and that resonates with your buyer
instantly, you have a good chance of selling your product.

You must try to conjure up a mood and spirit that says 'this is what my label is
about'. Just one look should tell your buyer whether your label is feminine, edgy,

*Men's tailoring department
at Harrods*

sophisticated or sporty. Your marketing materials – lookbooks, websites, catwalk shows – should reinforce the message of your product.

Clare Watson, freelance stylist, says:

'When labels are first starting out, I particularly like seeing small collections that are well thought-out and very together, as they are the ones that leave a lasting impression. Time after time, I see new designers who attempt to do a bit of everything to cover all areas that leaves everyone feeling confused about their style. Once you have established yourself with a style, then is the time to add new ideas that will then be far more easily accepted.'

Individuality

Try to create a USP that allows you to stand out from the crowd and gives buyers a reason to buy you. It sounds easy, but with so much competition it can be hard to be different yet still sellable. Exclusive fabrics, unique cuts, specialised trimmings, bold use of colour and selling price are all examples of ways to distinguish your product, and designing for a niche market can often be a way of ensuring that something is unique.

Commerciality

You want buyers to buy your product for their store and consumers to buy from the store to ensure reorders. Most shops will want to have sold 70 per cent of your stock before sale season comes around. (This is called the 'sell-through rate' and is always expressed as a percentage. 'Net sales' refers to the same thing, in absolute numbers. A low sell-through rate is one factor that may determine whether a shop stops buying your product line. You may be given a couple of seasons to improve sales and educate customers about your label, but most buyers will not want to give up valuable rail space to a line that does not bring a good return.) You need to know what is and isn't commercially viable for your market and incorporate this into your product. Good research can help. Once you start to build your stockist list you will get feedback from buyers about what their customers think, with ideas for adjusting your product to increase the potential for sales. It can be quite a challenge to create something both unique and sellable, but this is what successful fashion labels do.

Kat and Oz Aalam, of London boutique Damsel, say:

'[We] offer something different style-wise and take into account how practical our clients are! Dry-clean-only tops for the daytime don't work for us as most of our clients have kids! You also cannot underestimate the WOW factor. People will find a way to pay for something they absolutely love so it's got to be different and grab their attention! The high street's offer is now so competitive that boutiques like ours find it harder and harder to compete on price so we need to offer something to our customer that they can't get on the high street for a third of the cost.

'Price-points are also important – while my sister and I appreciate why beadwork, fabrics and design features justify high prices, we also know that we probably can't sell tops over £170/£180 or dresses over £300. That's just our market.'

Fashion accessories label Knomo were one of the first UK brands to introduce designer laptop bags into the market, instantly giving themselves a unique selling point

Quality

A good brand image is all about creating good feeling between yourself and your customer base, especially at the higher price points. It doesn't matter how great your samples looked and how many orders you have taken – if your quality is poor you will fail.

Customers won't buy your product if poor workmanship means the clothes look bad, and they won't buy your product again if quality becomes an issue after purchase. You need to spend as much time getting this right as you do on the design (see Chapter 10).

Value for Money

It doesn't matter how much you are charging for your product – people love to feel they are getting something special. Whether it is a bargain at the price or a bit of pure indulgence and luxury, you need to make your customer feel that they got a really good deal.

Expensive purchases can lead to 'cognitive dissonance' – a fear that you haven't made the right decision. You can combat this with product that offers fantastic design, quality, price and a USP. PR and marketing play a major role at this

Designers like Caroline Charles work hard to maintain a consistent message throughout their collections so that their customers can recognise the designer's handwriting season after season

point. The more your customers see your label in the press, the more they will be reassured that they have made the right purchase (see Chapter 12).

Consistency and Development

Having worked hard to develop a signature, you must maintain the identity of your label across the seasons, offering a consistent product range from which the buyers can select. Areas for key consideration in maintaining consistency include: design, fit, fabric and use of colour, with a strong emphasis on quality and price. There is nothing worse for a buyer who picks up your label one season than to find that you have completely changed the offer for the following season.

However, you still need to develop your collection from season to season, depending on how the market and trends are moving. Small boutique buyers know that their customer base is limited and, as a result, may be able to sell only so many of a given style. If you are offering the same style season after season there may soon be few customers to buy it. You need to be aware of the trends and how these can be adapted to key sellers within a range, moving the collection on and keeping it fresh, while keeping your signature recognisable.

Balance and Choice

How will your final collection look sitting on a rail in a store? Will it make sense to the customer? Does it have hanger appeal? You need to make sure that you create a balanced collection with enough width and depth or, alternatively, a single product with a strong identity. All the styles in a collection must work together to create a story and provide understandable options to the buyer.

Range Planning

Building a balanced range requires good range planning, which will deliver the right amount of choice and quantity within each collection. It combines your design budget and design/selling strategy to create a shopping list for the store buyer. It's about product selection and turning individual products into a commercially viable sample range. It is a key stage in the development of your collection.

The Range Width

The number of different styles/shapes you are going to offer will depend on your selling strategy, price point and type of product. The more styles you have on offer the greater the choice for the buyer, but it may be wise to limit the number of options you offer initially so as to keep costs to a minimum. You can sometimes deliver greater choice if you limit your product categories. You might decide to specialise in dresses and offer a choice of ten different styles, or you might want a denim range that initially focuses on six different cuts of jean. This not only gives you a choice within a product category but immediately gives you a signature that a buyer can easily recognise.

If, however, you want to create a full range, you may find your number of styles increasing rapidly. Remember that each style added means another pattern to be cut, with an increase in cost and more minimums to meet when it comes to the production run (see the next chapter).

Schumacher started out with five key pieces and Karen Walker with just one.

The Range Depth

You can produce every style in its own unique fabric, print or colourway. However, for a start-up label, this can often lead to difficulties in meeting the minimum order requirements of your fabric suppliers. Every style you develop will need to sell well on its own to ensure that you will be able to go into production with it. Too much variation in fabric and colour can also make your collection look disjointed and confuse the buyer.

When developing your collection you need to consider 'hanger appeal'. In other words, how your collection will look when sitting together en masse

By using the same colour and fabric options across a number of styles you can create 'stories' within your range, making it easier for buyers to comprehend and for you to meet your minimums.

The Price Architecture

Your market research should have given you a good starting point to work out the price that you can sell your product for. Remember that you will usually sell more of your lower-priced goods and your sample range should reflect this by offering a larger selection of pieces at the lower prices and fewer as the price increases. For instance, a basic camisole might be offered in four or five colourways, while a more elaborate party dress might just come in one or two.

Make a Template

Before you start the actual illustrative design process, sit down and work out a template. This should include the total number of pieces you are going to sample with a breakdown of styles, fabric and colour options as well as price points. Although you may have plenty of time with your first collection to get everything the way you want it, you will quickly find that once you are selling and overseeing the production, delivery and day-to-day running of a business, design time will be limited. A good template can help focus your designing and save time in the long run. It can also be a quick check to see how balanced your range is before you start spending on developing your samples.

Ultimately, good range planning is about predicting what your stockists will buy from you and the price point they will expect. It is about developing a range that is well balanced in colour, fabric and price, cohesive in its number of options – tops or bottoms – and offers a strong statement when hung in a store.

It is an ongoing exercise and you should analyse sales on a product-by-product basis season after season. It may well take a few seasons for you to work out exactly what your ideal range should be, but the faster you do so the less money you will waste, the more stockists you will pick up and the greater your chance of success.

Style Name	Rose print silk crêpe	Black silk crêpe	Red silk crêpe	Polka-dot print silk chiffon	Tulip print cotton	White cotton	Summer blue cotton	Cashmere cream knit	Cashmere black knit	Totals	Price RRP £
Mini cocktail dress	X	X		X						3	145.00
Maxi dress	X		X	X						3	190.00
Summer dress					X	X	X			3	95.00
Shirt dress					X		X			2	85.00
Backless cami	X	X		X						3	80.00
Party cami		X	X							2	95.00
Tunic	X		X	X						3	110.00
Buttoned-up shirt					X	X	X			3	65.00
Halter top		X		X						2	75.00
Summer knit								X	X	2	130.00
Summer short						X	X			2	45.00
Skinny trouser						X	X			2	75.00
Wrap skirt	X		X							2	110.00
Scarf	X			X	X					3	30.00
Totals	6	4	4	6	4	4	5	1	1	35	

When developing your subsequent collections it is important to analyse what has and hasn't worked from the previous season. One way to do this is to undertake a SWOT analysis.

SWOT Analysis

Strengths: What has worked well in the season? Why?
Weaknesses: What hasn't worked well in the season? Why?
Opportunities: What can you do to improve the performance of your label? How can you turn your weaknesses into strengths?
Threats: What outside factors could threaten your label?

Function, Fashionability and Added Value

Product developers often look at the overall impact a product will have on their chosen market by focusing on the three key areas of function, fashionability and added value. These can also be helpful for any small fashion label to think about and measure their product range against.

Function

Determine from the start what function your product will serve. People buy clothes for a purpose and by meeting the needs of the customer you are more likely to sell greater quantities. Therefore, if you are developing a range of winter coats, will they be warm? If you are developing swimwear for the beach, will it protect the modesty of the wearer when wet? And, most importantly, will your product make your customers feel confident and good about themselves?

Fashionability

Depending on how fashion-conscious your target customer is and where they fit in the trend hierarchy you will need to pitch the styling, shape, colour, fabric, print and trims of your product accordingly. It is sometimes easier to be a bit behind the trends when developing your range, as you can see what the fashion leaders have already developed and tweak your range to suit (see Chapter 11).

Added Value

This may come from the product itself through the use of unique fabrics, superb fit and exquisite trims as well as the unexpected – a printed pocket lining; a matching purse within a clutch bag. However, added value can also come from the profile of the designer or brand and the customer's perception of you. Press and advertising will help to develop your label's profile, increasing the added value placed on buying one of your pieces. Do not underestimate the added value of great design.

Customer Impact Diagram

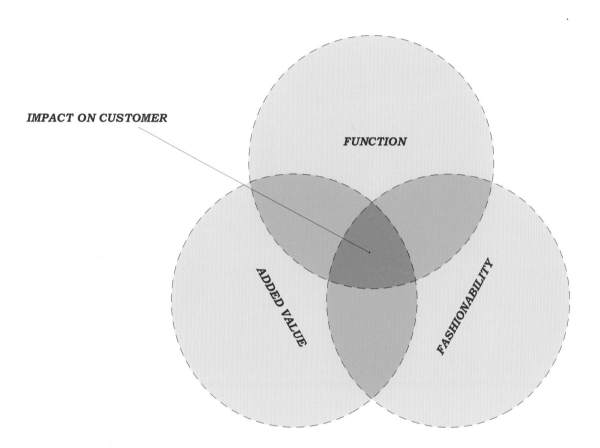

IMPACT ON CUSTOMER

FUNCTION

ADDED VALUE

FASHIONABILITY

TASK

Develop your own product-range template

Start off by determining the function of your product and your customer's profile. Then limit yourself to a number of pieces in your collection (20 to 30 may be a good starting point for this exercise) before moving on to decide on styles and colourways. Add rough guideline retail price points. Look back over your template to see if you have balanced the range. Have you used each colourway enough times and are there options for each style? Does your price architecture work?

Chapter 10: Getting it Made

*H*ow and where to get your product made is often the most daunting part of setting up your own fashion label. Simply put, finding a manufacturer to make the product to the quality and quantity you require and at a price that makes your business plan profitable can be tough. This chapter will introduce you to the process.

Manufacturing Options

It is important to understand the technicalities of the manufacturing process so that you will then be in a better position to make the decision that best suits your product and overall supply chain. Your manufacturing options include:

In House:
✖ Common for fashion start-ups where the designer is technically trained in pattern cutting and machining
✖ Allows for very small quantities to be developed
✖ You keep close control over quality
✖ Can be problematic when larger orders have to be produced
✖ You are responsible for sourcing all of the components.

Cottage Industry:
✖ Outsources the sampling/production of your product to technically proficient skilled labour (pattern cutters/seamstresses), usually working from home
✖ Can be charged by the hour, by the day or by the pattern/garment/accessory
✖ Allows very small numbers of each style to be developed
✖ If sourced locally, you can maintain close control over the quality
✖ Can be problematic when larger orders have to be produced
✖ You are responsible for sourcing all of the components.

CMT (Cut, Make, Trim):
✖ Outsources sampling/production to a production unit with a number of technical workers who will cut, make and add trims
✖ Allows for smaller production runs and more potential for larger runs where needed
✖ You are responsible for sourcing all of the components.

Full Package Manufacturers:
✖ Outsources sampling/production of product to a factory that will give you a fully-costed product including patterns, fabrics and CMT
✖ May provide sourcing services for fabrics and trims as well as developing garment labels/swing tickets

Image by David Hardy

✖ Product is delivered to you ready to be shipped to customers
✖ Depending on the size of the factory it usually allows for greater numbers to
  be produced.

Production Process

While the type of product you have designed will determine the production
process, there are key stages that are common to most fashion products.

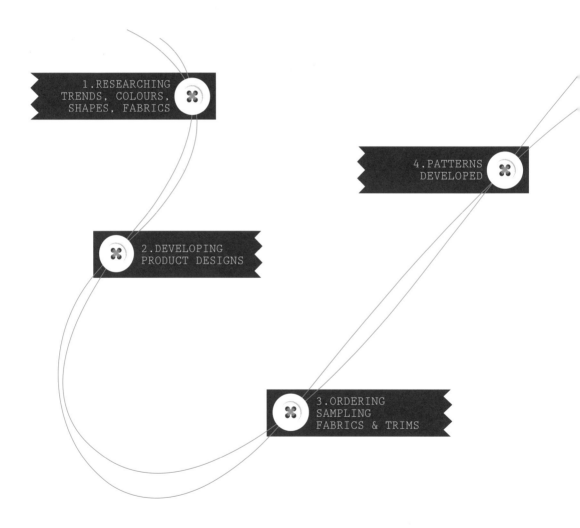

1. RESEARCHING TRENDS, COLOURS, SHAPES, FABRICS

2. DEVELOPING PRODUCT DESIGNS

3. ORDERING SAMPLING FABRICS & TRIMS

4. PATTERNS DEVELOPED

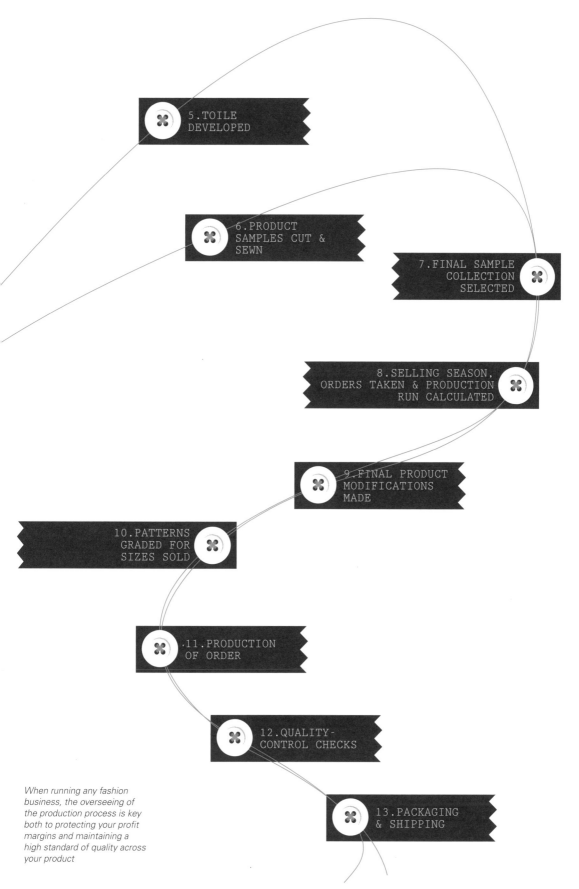

5.TOILE DEVELOPED

6.PRODUCT SAMPLES CUT & SEWN

7.FINAL SAMPLE COLLECTION SELECTED

8.SELLING SEASON, ORDERS TAKEN & PRODUCTION RUN CALCULATED

9.FINAL PRODUCT MODIFICATIONS MADE

10.PATTERNS GRADED FOR SIZES SOLD

·11.PRODUCTION OF ORDER

12.QUALITY-CONTROL CHECKS

13.PACKAGING & SHIPPING

When running any fashion business, the overseeing of the production process is key both to protecting your profit margins and maintaining a high standard of quality across your product

A designer's initial sketch or illustration will be turned into a technical specification drawing before being given to the manufacturer for the final garment to be produced

Research Trends, Colours, Shapes, Fabrics

Chapter 8 showed that trends in fashion can come from many sources: get tuned into as many different ones as possible.

Develop Product Designs

When going into production with manufacturers you will need to supply technical drawings – 'specification drawings' or 'specs' – to give to the manufacturer on a specification sheet (see above). It is essential that these are accurate, or the first sample will not be as you intended and can lead to additional costs.

Order Sampling Fabrics and Trims

One of the keys to the success of your product line is your ability to source the correct fabrics and trimmings in the right quantities and at the right price. A full package manufacturer will usually offer assistance in sourcing fabrics. Many designers, however, choose to source their fabrics directly to ensure a greater choice, whilst others develop their own fabrics to guarantee uniqueness.

Tips for Shopping at a Fabric Fair

==

Suzanna Crabb *– Creative Director of designer womenswear label Suzanna*

✖ *Determine the trends you are interested in before visiting, and use the fair as confirmation of trends as well as inspiration for new ones.*

✖ *Keep a shopping list of approximately what you are looking for – denim, printed silk or jersey, for example – as the fairs are vast and allocate certain areas to certain fabrics.*

✖ *Take business cards.*

✖ *Try to visit a fair on the last (or first) day, when it should be quieter, to access stands and have the pick of the cuttings.*

===

Fabric fairs and fabric agents are two common ways to source fabric for your product line. The large international shows, such as Premier Vision and Texworld in Paris, attract large numbers of exhibitors and visitors. Fabric agents work with fabric suppliers on your behalf.

It is advisable as a start-up to order your production fabric only when you know your sales quantities. Many bigger designers will make predictions at the beginning of the season based on previous seasons' sales, but it is a big risk for a small label.

Cut Patterns

The first step in making your samples will be to cut the patterns – these will form the basis of the fit. Poor fit is one of the biggest reasons for fashion product not selling, therefore it is important that either you or the person you outsource to is experienced.

Make Toiles

Toiles are made after the patterns have been cut. Before the first sample is sewn using the correct fabric there is usually a need for a toile – a sample of a garment made in a cheap material so that alterations may be made before the garment is made up in the correct material.

Toiles will often have to be adjusted before first samples are produced

Cut and Sew Product Samples

Once the sample fabric has been selected and the first pattern cut it is time to put the product together. Your sample collection is your key tool for both selling and promoting your collection, and must be perfect. If you have overseen the preceding steps carefully there should be no reason for samples to be different from your initial designs, although when outsourcing sampling without overseeing it, adjustments and modifications will often be necessary.

Select Final Sample Collection

Before you go into your selling period you may need to edit your collection. When your samples come back you may find that individual pieces are not quite working and are reducing the overall impact of the line. It may be best to omit these from your final range.

Take Orders and Calculate the Production Run

At the end of the sales season and when you have confirmed your orders (see Chapter 11) you will need to calculate your production run. This will tell you exactly how many pieces per style and colourway you will need to produce and in what sizes. This will in turn determine the exact quantities of fabric and trims required. A full package manufacturer will have a merchandiser who will take your production run and calculate quantities of fabric and trims. If you are undertaking the production in-house, or through a cottage industry or a CMT, it will be your responsibility to calculate everything correctly. You must be careful not to under- or over-order. There are software packages that can help with these calculations.

As well as a spreadsheet of the overall production run, it is also a good idea to hand over a docket or cutting ticket to the manufacturer. This is similar to your earlier specification sheet with all the product details, but includes the quantities of each size going into production.

Make Final Product Modifications

When the sales period has ended you may need to make some final modifications to your product. You must communicate these changes quickly and clearly to your production team. This can mean changing spec drawings or making notes on existing specification sheets. Don't rely on simply telling the team what the changes are. They need to be documented and made available as hard copy.

Grade Patterns for Sizes Sold

Before you began selling your collection you should have decided what sizes you would offer. You need to grade your original patterns up and down to develop patterns for all the sizes you are going into production with.

Produce the Order

You will need to have the role of production manager firmly in place to oversee the actual production of the final pieces. In the early days you will probably

When starting out it is common for most designers to have to undertake all of their own quality control checks as well as packaging and shipping out their orders

undertake this yourself. You will have agreed delivery dates (see Chapter 11) with your buyers and you will be expected to deliver on time and with good quality. This means keeping on top of your production team. Obviously the further away your team is geographically, the harder this can be. Establish a realistic production timeline with your production unit so that you can work out on a weekly and monthly basis if you are on schedule. It is your job to make sure the schedule is adhered to.

Make Quality-Control Checks

Poor quality can be the undoing of new labels. The only real way of guaranteeing quality is to check and double check every single piece.

Your quality-control checks should be happening throughout the production process to minimise any potential problems. If you are finding faults and having to reproduce the pieces you may jeopardise your delivery date.

Package and Ship

When selling your collection you will have to agree shipping terms with your buyers. It is most common for small labels to place the responsibility for shipping the goods with the stores. This is to protect yourself if anything goes wrong once the goods have left your studio. Make this clear in your terms and conditions when selling. Stores will, however, often issue instructions on how they expect the goods to be delivered. This can include asking for garments to come hanging or flat-packed. Department stores often have very specific guidelines that need to be followed and you will usually have to book in the delivery with them ahead of time. Failure to do this can often result in goods being sent back to you and the cost charged against your order.

If you are selling overseas and have agreed to sell the product at a 'landed price', then not only does the responsibility of shipment rest with you but so does the cost of any import duty and tax. Make sure you have costed this into your selling price before agreeing to the terms.

If you are manufacturing your product overseas you will have to arrange delivery of the goods to you. It is worth establishing a relationship with a freight company who will organise the shipment, including paperwork and insurance. It is also worth seeing if you can arrange a credit period with your freight company. This means that they will usually initially cover any import duty and tax and then invoice you for the shipping charge plus tax and duty, giving you a bit of time to pay it off.

Minimums

A minimum is the lowest threshold you can order from a supplier. The minimums exist because the work involved in producing smaller quantities often makes them unprofitable. So, in order to make sure an order is worthwhile and leads to a workable profit margin, a supplier puts a minimum order on goods purchased. Minimums most commonly apply to fabric/trim orders and manufacturing quantities.

Minimums can vary hugely, and for fabric orders may range from 20 to 2,000 metres, depending on the supplier, but for the designer sector it will usually start at around 200 metres. For manufacturing you will find CMTs who can offer you anything from one piece per style, usually at a higher price, to full package manufacturers who might start at around 500 pieces per style, but with a significant decrease in cost per unit.

Ways Around Minimums

✖ *Offer to pay more:* Although suppliers put minimum orders in place to maximise their profitability you may find that the unit price increase for orders under the minimum may not be that high.

✖ *Ask for stock goods:* Most manufacturers and suppliers will hold on to stock of fabric and finished product, and you may find that minimums are much more relaxed when the stock has already been produced. If you cannot get the exact fabric you require, ask if there is anything similar in stock fabrics. Depending on how unique your finished product design is, you may find that a supplier has a similar standard product that you can add to.

✖ *Tack your order on:* If you are not able to meet the minimum, ask whether there is a chance of including your order at the end of another major order.

✖ *Creative design:* By cutting down on the styles within your range and offering fewer colour options you may meet the minimums required. Otherwise, you could buy a large amount of white fabric and dye it yourself. It is common for designers to make a name for themselves in one fabric for this very reason.

Exclusivity

Suppliers may not be keen to give you exclusivity on a small order. Without exclusivity another major player may come in and get exclusive rights, leaving you hanging out to dry without any product or fabric. You may also find that somebody else is selling exactly the same product as yours at a cheaper price.

Exclusivity tends to become a major issue around recognisable characteristics. Printed fabric is one example and is obviously something that can distinguish your collection from that of a competitor.

Developing your own fabric prints can be a good option, but if you are buying the fabric or product ready-made, ask if anybody else has bought that particular one.

For footwear designer Gil Carvalho, Italy was the only option when it came to the location for manufacturing his shoes

Sourcing a Manufacturer

As your sales increase so will the need for you to find a more sizable manufacturing base.

There are many things to consider when outsourcing your production. Fashion start-ups often get themselves into difficulties by not allowing themselves enough time to source their production properly. Take time to consider all of the following:

Location

In an ideal world your manufacturer would be just around the corner from your studio. However, if this is not feasible, start looking as locally as possible. The further you are geographically from your manufacturer the harder communication becomes and the more difficult it is to drop in for a meeting. Sometimes your place of manufacture is dictated by the type of product or even the image you want to project.

As footwear designer Gil Carvalho says, 'Luxury ladies' shoes are synonymous with Italian production so there was really no choice. We only had to choose the factory most suited to our needs as a company.'

If your manufacturer is overseas it's a good idea to take on an agent to oversee the production process. Agents can also help in the sourcing of factories and often work with a number of manufacturers.

Websites such as *www.alibaba.com* offer worldwide sourcing of manufacturers, but you should use them only for initial introductions. You will need to do your research and visit suppliers to make sure they are right for you. You can also contact trade associations in different countries for a list of potential manufacturers.

===

TASKS

1   Identify three fashion labels whose quality and finish you believe to be excellent. Go to their stockists and look at the garment labels to see where their production is done. Search online or contact the embassy or trade association of that country and ask for a list of manufacturers.

2   Look in your local business directory and make a list of seamstresses, tailors and dry-cleaners. Call around for their rates. Even if you work with a big manufacturer it is always good to have these skills on hand in case of an emergency.

===

Materials, Machinery and Production Techniques

You should be working with a manufacturer specialising in the fabrics you are using and with a supplier who can give you access to all you need. Ask for a sample to be made up to demonstrate the standard of workmanship before committing yourself. You may have to pay for this but it will save you a great deal of money and heartbreak in the long run.

If, however, you are bringing fabrics and trims from one country to another, you will need to check the taxes on each of the products being imported. Some countries place very high taxes on the import of certain raw materials to protect their own domestic market.

Quality

The quality of your product is a big factor in the success of your label, and the higher the price point the better the quality should be. In different countries expectations of what constitutes high quality can differ, and this is where samples play an important role. Your sample should be an indicator of the quality you expect when you go into production.

Lead Times

Having agreed delivery dates with your stores you need to be confident that your manufacturer can deliver to you on time. Lead times can vary from factory to factory, with many asking for 60 to 90 days. This will include getting fabrics and trims delivered to them. However, the delivery date will be the date on which the goods are ready to leave them, not the date they will arrive with you. You will then have to factor in time for shipping.

Quantity

Can the manufacturer deliver the quantities you need at the prices you require?

Reliability

You will need your manufacturer to be reliable. When they set a delivery date the goods will need to be ready; when you set a quality standard they must stick to it. You also want to make sure they are a stable business and are going to be around to produce your production run. Ask for references from their other clients.

Negotiation

A manufacturer is not going to make a lot of money out of you until your order quantities really start to rise. As a result you are not the most attractive proposition, and you will find that large numbers of manufacturers will not even entertain working with you. You need to convince manufacturers that you are important and that they should look after your production as well as possible. To do this you can:

✖ Increase your order quantity
✖ Reorder
✖ Pay on time
✖ Let the manufacturer know when you are in the media; they gain kudos by working with a successful company.

Terms and Conditions

It is important to agree terms and conditions up front, ideally in the form of a contract, although manufacturers are often reluctant to sign contracts and you will have to rely on verbal agreements or email confirmations. You should look for the following in writing:

Full Manufacturing Agreement

Covers order quantities, shipment, payment, insurance, quality and delivery dates. It should also prevent the manufacturer selling on your designs to a third party without first discussing it with you and obtaining your agreement.

Agreement for Provision of a Sample

Will you pay for sampling or will it be free if you guarantee to go into production for a certain number of units? Who owns the rights to the sample if you choose not to go into production with the manufacturer?

Confidentiality or Non-Disclosure Agreement

This states that the manufacturer agrees not to discuss your product with anyone or show it to anyone outside of your and the manufacturer's business. As a small label a manufacturer may well work with you for the kudos your name can bring and may want to show off your product to their bigger, more mass-produced clients.

Price and Payment

The manufacturer should usually give you a rough estimate of price based on the specification drawings, then a completed price per style once samples have been made. If you are working with a full package manufacturer this price should be inclusive of everything apart from delivery. You should negotiate this price, as manufacturers will often quote an initial price, expecting you to come in with a lower counter-offer. It is also important to agree the payment terms.

Delivery

Most manufacturers will expect you to look after the shipping of your product from their factory, especially if this involves import or export duty and tax. Make sure you know what your unit price does and doesn't include.

Common Delivery Terms

==

Ex Factory: *The price includes only the cost of the goods and you are responsible for all freight, insurance, duties and tax incurred in shipping the product. Ownership of the goods transfers to you once the product has been picked up from the factory.*

FOB (Free On Board): *The goods will be deemed to be delivered to you at the point that the goods pass the ship's rail. Obviously, this will normally be as the goods are swung on to the ship in their container.*

CIF (Cost, Insurance and Freight): *The manufacturer is providing a price inclusive of the cost of goods, the insurance for their journey to their destination port/unloading point, and the cost of whichever method of freight is being used to transport the goods to you.*

CFR or C&F (Cost and Freight): *The manufacturer is providing a price which includes the cost of the goods and of the freight, but not insurance.*

LDP (Landed Duty Paid): *The price includes goods, insurance, freight and the duties and quotas associated with importing the product.*

==

Manufacturing will be an ongoing process for your fashion label and is therefore something you need to get your head around quickly. It can be the most time-consuming aspect of running your business, especially if you are creating a new and exciting collection two, three or even four times a year. You will find that at the same time as making sure samples are arriving on time and to specification, the production of the previous season's orders will need overseeing and sending out.

Give yourself 12 to 18 months to sort out your entire supply chain so that you are confident when you take your product to market for the first time that you have an infrastructure in place that will allow you to maximise the potential of your business. Don't be in a rush and never assume that your production will take care of itself.

Production Calendar (Northern Hemisphere)

Month	Spring/Summer 2010	Autumn/Winter 2010
March 2009	Research fabric Start designs	
April 2009	Select fabrics Order fabrics	
May 2009	Create patterns Begin sampling	
June 2009	Collections developed	
July 2009	Establish production plan Finish sampling	
August 2009	Sales season begins	
September 2009	Collections shown Sales continue	Research fabric Start designs
October 2009	Order books close	Select fabrics Order fabrics
November 2009	Production materials ordered Production starts	Create patterns Begin sampling
December 2009	Oversee production	Collections developed
January 2010	Oversee production	Establish production plan Finish sampling
February 2010	Production arrives Deliver to stores	Sales season begins
March 2010	Continuation of deliveries Chasing of monies owed	Collections shown Sales continue
April 2010		Order books close
May 2010		Production materials ordered Production starts
June 2010		Oversee production
July 2010		Oversee production
August 2010		Production arrives Deliver to stores
September 2010		Continuation of deliveries Chasing of monies owed

Case Study: Caroline Charles

Caroline Charles has been one of the UK's leading womenswear fashion designers since setting up her label in the 1960s. Over the past 40 years she has established the Caroline Charles brand throughout the world by offering modern, easy, useful, lasting and ageless designs to an international client list of women with a hectic working, travel and social life. Throughout an illustrious career that has seen her dress pop stars, film stars and royalty, Caroline has been at the forefront of the British fashion industry, receiving, in her fortieth year of operation, an OBE for services to the fashion industry.

Caroline's vision and creative approach have remained steadfast since the conception of the label. She has a true belief in the style that she represents and is a perfectionist in every detail of the production, display and selling of the products. Admitting to being 'tremendously driven', she is hands-on in every aspect of her business, and is quick to point out she has the backing of 'the best team in London'.

Caroline designs three collections each season, all of which show off her love of textiles, cut and finish. Her Caroline Charles London line is dedicated to celebrations, parties and performances. The Caroline Collection moves the focus to jeans, suede leather, embroidery, T-shirts, knitwear, skirts and shirts, whilst the Caroline Charles Studio line offers a limited edition collection focusing on evening wear made in luxurious fabrics, many of which have been embroidered and beaded by hand.

Each range offers the Caroline Charles customer something different and Caroline works hard to maintain the brand's identity and USPs by focusing on specialist fabrics, textures, weaves, embroidery, beading and novelties.

Although stocked in leading boutiques and department stores around the world, Caroline is a keen advocate of retailing her own product: 'In your own retail space you are able to decorate/merchandise your clothes to their best advantage, while with wholesaling you rely on others to express their taste.' Caroline opened her first retail store in the 1970s on Beauchamp Place, Knightsbridge, in the heart of London, and since then has used a successful retail strategy to develop her business.

She says, 'The right time to start retailing is when you feel the customers will follow', and that to deliver a successful product you should offer 'design for the customers' needs and tempt them with extras – think in terms of colour groups, occasions, travel, weather, etc.'

Caroline has opened stores in a number of locations but has always tried to 'get a shop with the highest footfall/passing trade that budget will allow', and says it is important to 'be as close to similarly-priced products as possible.' She has negotiated a number of leases for her retail premises and believes that the best are 25-year leases, with breakpoints after one, two and five years. 'The breakpoints give the opportunity to take your business elsewhere if the location is not working.' Sometimes negotiating 'a turnover rent can also work well, i.e. pay the landlord 10 per cent of the annual turnover for two years, then negotiate a fixed sum based on those figures.'

Caroline sees getting the right staff to run her shops as being as important as the product. 'Employ people who enjoy selling and who are very friendly and helpful. Natural shopkeepers love dressing the shop and moving the product around each week, including window-dressing.' She also says it is important that terms and conditions for customer service and staff should be clearly thought-out. Within this she includes dress codes for staff – they play an important role in determining the brand image and therefore need to look the part.

Caroline believes it is important to set 'sales targets against your budget and year on year make a percentage increase to those targets'. However, she is not one to say no to a great find for a piece to sell in the shop and is quick to say, 'Do not resist some irresistible accessory!'

One last essential ingredient for Caroline's retail success to date has been 'good PR and a good mailing list'. These, she says, are 'essential to keep reminding people that you are open!'

Caroline Charles is one of the UK's top fashion designers and has built a successful business over the past 40 years, with a strong emphasis on her own retail outlets

*S*elling is about talking to people and building trusting, long-lasting relationships. People buy from people they like – depending on your selling strategy you may get only two chances a year in which to meet with buyers, so it is important to get it right first time. You must also be able to talk about your own product convincingly. This chapter looks at all aspects of fashion wholesaling and retailing, at the potential for licensing agreements, and at all the administrative details that are part and parcel of the selling process.

The Sales Window

Before you work out when exactly you will be undertaking the sales of your collection you must have decided on your sales strategy. Will you be wholesaling, retailing or both?

The Wholesale Sales Window

For most fashion wholesalers the selling period will be dictated by the spring/summer and autumn/winter collections, with two sales windows a year lasting between two and four months each. This is when the store buyers will have their budget for the new collections. If you can replenish your goods throughout the season, allowing stores to reorder, additional selling periods will be available to you. The dates for the menswear and womenswear collections are slightly different, with the men's collections usually being shown first.

Pre-collections are presented up to three months ahead of the main seasonal catwalk presentations and are becoming increasingly important to the economic survival of the sector. They are often slightly more wearable and affordable than the catwalk collections – a response by the designer market to the success achieved by the fast-fashion model of the high street. Many high-end buyers do not want to wait for the seasonal catwalk shows to take place before placing orders, as deliveries of these collections often arrive too late in the season for their core customers. As the high-end shopper is usually keen to have the clothes before anyone else, buyers know that they need to get the collections in-store just before the shopping season begins in earnest. Pre-collections allow the store to sell great designer collections earlier, whilst giving the designer the creative freedom to keep the catwalk collection as inspirational as possible.

Buying appointment at Bread & Butter trade fair, Barcelona

Wholesale Sales Calendar

Pre-collection autumn/winter	December
Main collection autumn/winter	January through to April
Pre-collection spring/summer	July
Main collection spring/summer	August through to November

Depending on your product you may also find that a market exists for year-round sales, and your stockists want the opportunity to come back to you from time to time to replenish their stock. This means that you may have to hold some stock or else have a very tight supply chain with short lead times.

The Retail Sales Window

The retail sales window is also driven by seasons, and stock should arrive in stores three to six months later than the wholesale window. For the designer sector it is usual for the spring/summer collections to arrive in stores around January/February, whilst the autumn/winter collections hit the rails in August/September. The more mass market your product the greater the opportunity for shorter but more frequent sales seasons, when the product hits the shop floor at exactly the time of year it is intended to be worn (see the fast fashion model on page 15).

Wholesaling

Fashion wholesalers sell goods to a third party who will sell the goods on to the consumer. If you will need a boutique or department store or an online market-place such as *www.net-a-porter.com* to sell your goods to the consumer, even if it is only a few pieces, you will be considered a wholesaler.

The biggest advantage of wholesaling is that you can limit your initial stock investment to the order quantities placed by stores. So, before you purchase your goods from your manufacturer you already know exactly how many pieces you will require, in which styles, colours and sizes.

The biggest disadvantage is that you are not getting the full retail value of your goods (see Chapter 13).

There are three main reasons why many fashion start-ups choose the wholesale route:

Limited funds: Fashion retailing can mean greater overheads, including investment in stock. Many new fashion labels simply cannot afford to retail.

Distribution: Wholesaling gives you the potential to be represented in hundreds of stores worldwide, making your label instantly accessible to many potential customers.

Credibility: An established retailer who chooses your label to be represented in their shop is telling customers that you are worthy of their attention.

Studio Sales

As a new fashion business, getting buyers to come to you can be tricky. Your lookbooks and other marketing materials (see Chapter 12) are there to entice the buyer into making an appointment with you. They serve as an introduction to your label and the new collection. However, buyers see hundreds of lookbooks each season, so you will need to build relationships with them by cold calling to introduce yourself, make sure they received your lookbook and marketing materials, and ask for an appointment.

Make sure your studio sends out the right message and is presented well, and that the collection looks fantastic. Be tidy and be prepared – fresh flowers always look good. Offer the buyers a drink and make sure you have enough seating. Making them welcome and comfortable is an important part of building a good and lasting relationship.

Rejection is part and parcel of the selling game. Established stores may not be looking for any new collections. Even if they are looking to drop one or two lines they have hundreds of collections from which to choose. You may be lucky and have the right product at the right time, but for most new fashion labels it's a case of slowly building your reputation with these stores until the time is right for them to buy. Don't take a 'no' personally, and remember that it doesn't mean 'no' forever. After a few seasons, when the buyer has seen your product and press for a while, they may be ready to stock you. Be persistent.

Exhibitions

Exhibitions give buyers a good opportunity to see many different collections under one roof in a short period of time. Choosing the right exhibition is key – you can't afford to spend money on the wrong one. Do your research. Which exhibitions do your competitors attend? Ask the organisers for their exhibitor and buyer attendance lists from previous seasons. Talk with other fashion businesses that have attended in previous seasons. You don't want to sign up for an exhibition based solely on the previous exhibitor lists only to find that poor buyer attendance means those exhibitors are no longer showing.

Exhibitions play a massive role in the sales strategy of most wholesale fashion labels. Research exhibitions thoroughly and work out which one is best for your label before committing yourself

The exhibition organisers decide which fashion labels participate and they will work hard to protect the reputation of their event. You must present yourself professionally. Any pre-launch press you have achieved will be impressive. If you already have stockists you will be bringing buyers to the exhibition. It may take a few seasons to be accepted, especially into one of the bigger exhibitions with established brands. However, once you have been accepted you will need to think about how you will present your collection.

You must keep to a tight budget in the first season. This means not taking on too big a stand. However, you will need a stand that is large enough to show off your collection in a professional and visually stimulating manner. Make sure you have enough rail space – but not too much. Most exhibitions have minimum stand sizes. Accessories labels can often take a smaller stand than clothing labels, as their product often takes up less space, especially if it is jewellery. Check with the organisers.

You must present your collection professionally – make sure your hangers are all the same and attach swing tickets to each item.

Try to create an enticing space that leaves the buyer some room for interpretation. You want them to come on to your stand with an open mind. There will probably be something there for them whether their store has a minimalist or French boudoir theme.

Send out lookbooks with details of where you will be exhibiting and which stand you will be on. Many buyers go to exhibitions to meet with their existing customers rather than to look for new labels. If they do have a look around the exhibition they should already have been introduced to your label. This increases the likelihood of name and product recognition and may persuade them to have a look though your collection.

Buyers from big stores often travel in packs. They will know exactly what they are looking for and will attend specific shows, like Magic in Las Vegas, where they are guaranteed to see a number of interesting brands relevant to their market

Position tables and chairs to maximise the potential of your space. The stand needs to be functional but exciting. A changing room can be very helpful for buyers who want to see how things fit. If you can, stretch your budget to a fit model (a model who is the perfect sample size for your product).

Types of Buyers

Buyers range from those who know what they want (department stores and established boutiques) to those just starting out, who can be a little overwhelmed. Others will be keen to buy but will need your guidance. Some buyers will be totally on your wavelength and love your collection whilst others will not be at all interested. You will also find some time-wasters who will go through the collection at length but never place an order. Don't allow anyone to take pictures of your collection before they place an order unless they are from a reputable store or have a press pass (after a few seasons you will recognise who's who). It is common for buyers to want to see you for a few seasons before placing their first order. They will want to see continuity and growth before making the decision to bring you on board.

Buyers will often give feedback, whether they are buying or not. It is worth listening to it, even if it's a little harsh. You will quickly find that different buyers will like and dislike different things, quite often contradicting each other on what needs to be changed. Write everything down. However, do not be ready to throw everything out the window and start again from scratch. Buyers will most often be talking about what is right for their specific customers and it may be that you have not met the right buyers yet. Being true to yourself and your creativity is an important part of establishing your label's identity.

Always get business cards from buyers and make a note on the back of when and where you met, together with any feedback.

Exhibiting Abroad

It is often recommended not to exhibit abroad until you have some revenue coming in to cover the additional costs. However, some young fashion businesses who do not do well in their domestic market do fantastically well in the overseas markets. Taking part in exhibitions abroad will often add credibility – telling a buyer that you exhibit in London, Paris, Milan and New York shows that you must already have achieved some success.

Talk to other designers about their experience and to the government department responsible for exporting and doing business in different countries. You may even be eligible for a grant.

The Art of Selling

==

Step 1: Set goals
You need clearly defined goals that are measurable over a specific timeframe. When setting your goals initially, consider your 'break-even' point and what revenue is needed to continue functioning. Break this down into a seasonal sales target. Later you can aim to increase last season's sales turnover by a specific amount.

Step 2: Prospecting
Prospecting is the process of looking for new leads to sell to. Continual research of new boutiques and stores is needed to maximise the number of potential customers. Allocate time to finding new customers as well as building up a database of loyal buyers.

Step 3: Qualifying
This is the art of sorting the qualified prospects from the unqualified. Out of your 20 new leads, which ones are truly ready now to buy your type of product at the price you are offering? By qualifying your prospects you will save a great deal of time, building relationships with potential new customers rather than chasing those that are not willing or able to buy.

Step 4: The sales process
The sales process is all about building a relationship of trust and a rapport between you and your buyers. People like doing business with people they like, especially in small businesses. Get them excited about some key pieces in the collection and build from there. When talking through your product, remember to sell the benefits in a way your buyer can appreciate and focus your questions to complement their business interests, whether it be style or the bottom line.

Step 5: Follow up
After the sale has been closed and the buyer has placed an order, following up the sale is imperative to building a long-term relationship. A note to say it was great meeting them, periodic calls to let them know how delivery is going, clippings of any press that has been achieved, will help to make buyers feel they have made the right choice. Once the goods have been delivered, it's always good to follow up and see if everything is ok and how the collection is selling.

==

TASKS

1 *Go to* www.5portlandplace.org.uk *and click on a calendar in the menu bar options to see all the fashion exhibitions taking place around the world. Identify exhibitions that might be suited to your product and investigate on the internet.*

2 *Come up with a list of ten successful similar labels that you would like to be sold next to. Check out their websites for their stockist lists and research boutiques and department stores to approach.*

==

Showrooms and Agents

If you feel that you are not the person to take on the selling of your collection you could hand it over to a showroom or an agent. A showroom will show your collection along with those of other designers, and an agent may take one or more collections to the buyers. Agents might also have a space to show the collection or even take a stand at exhibitions. They should have a list of already established clients, so you may be able to piggyback on someone else's relationship.

The showroom/agent does not purchase the product from you but merely meets new and existing stockists on your behalf. Most work on a commission basis, usually 10 per cent of all sales. The best payment option for you, and the most common, is for payment to be made following delivery of the goods to the store and after you have been paid.

You are responsible for distribution, and the showroom/agent will pass all the orders, contracts and shipping details to you.

Before taking you on, showrooms/agents have to feel confident that you will sell enough to make the relationship worthwhile. Quite often they will want to see that you have been trading for a few seasons and have picked up some stockists from which they can grow your business.

There are various agreements you can enter into with your showroom/agent. These can range from a simple handshake to establishing a formal joint venture. As neither party will be sure whether the relationship is going to last you are best leaving the joint venture to a later date, but a Heads of Agreement or an Exchange of Letters with a new showroom/agent is advisable. Ask your solicitor for advice.

Heads of Agreement/Exchange of Letters for Agents or Distributors

===

This should include the following:

✖ *Description of the products involved*
✖ *Agreed territory*
✖ *Timeframe*
✖ *Termination clauses – these need to be established at the beginning of the relationship when you and your representative are on good terms*
✖ *Review clauses – set dates for reviewing the agreement and state what will be reviewed*
✖ *Performance targets – could include sales quantities, numbers of customers, advertising campaigns, and so on.*

===

Distributors

Using a distributor is quite common when selling in overseas markets where language can be problematic. The distributor is your one and only client for the agreed region and places one big order with you, taking responsibility for managing the relationships with the stores, including delivery and payment. The distributor purchases the product from you and then sells it on, most often marking up your supply price (although in some cases they may negotiate a percentage of sales, ranging from 2 to 12 per cent, depending on your potential sales turnover), to cover additional in-market costs of ownership distribution and invoicing/debt-recovery. The distributor will be responsible for all after-sales service and will help pay for and undertake promotion and marketing of your collection in the agreed market.

Agency v Distributorship

===

Advantages of an agent:

✖ *Agents can have very good market expertise and their own ready-made client base*
✖ *An agent usually charges an agreed commission (around ten per cent on all sales), so selling costs are known in advance and can be built into pricing*
✖ *You usually pay an agent after the buyer has paid you*
✖ *You retain control over your branding as you are responsible for marketing and promotion.*

Disadvantages of an agent:

✖ *You are responsible for all deliveries of goods, which, if selling in many countries, can result in a relatively complex distribution process*
✖ *The agent is unlikely to be involved in funding promotional activity and does not usually undertake marketing or promotion of your product. Some agencies offer press and marketing services separately for a monthly retainer*
✖ *The credit risk falls to you; however, because you usually pay the agent after you have been paid, the agent may well follow up payment on your behalf.*

Advantages of a distributor:

✖ *You've got only one customer (the distributor)*
✖ *The distributor is responsible for the credit risk of all sales*
✖ *The distributor holds your stock in-market (i.e., in the sales territory for which they are responsible)*
✖ *The distributor helps pay for and undertakes marketing and promotion of your product in the market*
✖ *The distributor develops a customer base for your product.*

Disadvantages of a distributor:

✖ *They have complete control of the selling process; you have none*
✖ *The cost of selling through a distributor may force the product out of market competition – a distributor may add up to 50 per cent mark-up (or even more) to your product before it reaches the retailer*
✖ *You may not know who your customers are*
✖ *Because a distributor shares responsibility for marketing and promotion, you may not retain total control over the branding of your product*
✖ *Distributors who are wholesalers (rather than specialised master distributors) may not sell effectively to other wholesalers*
✖ *Your distributor may not have the sales force for new product introductions in larger markets*
✖ *Your distributor's time and attention may be spread over multiple products.*

==

Licensing Agreements

In a licence you, as the owner of the brand (the licensor) give another party (the licensee) permission to design, manufacture and market products using your brand, in exchange for a royalty. By doing so you will be able to expand your brand into other product categories in which you may have no manufacturing or sales expertise, and the licensee is able to add value to their product while gaining access to your loyal customer base. Many designer labels lend their names to a variety of products, with perfumes being the major money-spinner for fashion brands. Donna Karan, Ralph Lauren, Chanel, Alexander McQueen and Paul Smith all have a number of licensing agreements for the production and distribution of selected products.

Before entering into a licensing agreement you will need to consider, however, how much of your input is required and how much control you will retain. It can all depend on the agreement. The most serious caveat in a licensing agreement is undoubtedly the potential loss of control of quality, design, and marketing strategy.

You will need to show any contracts to your solicitor to make sure you are getting a good deal as well as doing enough to protect your brand.

Exclusivity

Stores may ask for a certain amount of exclusivity with your collection, ranging from total exclusivity (you sell only in their store), to regional exclusivity (you agree not to sell within a certain geographical area around their store). It is up

to you to determine how important the store is for you. If they have more than 100 outlets and you will be doing a lot of business with them, total exclusivity for a specific period of time may be an option. If you are a designer label you may want to maintain the exclusiveness of your product. Selling to too many stores in a small town may make your label too accessible and devalue the brand. On the other hand, you don't want to agree to anything that is not going to allow your business to develop a healthy client base and turnover. Think very carefully before agreeing any exclusivity.

The Paperwork

You will need to get all your paperwork ready for the selling season.

Order forms

When a buyer is ready to place an order you will need to have an order form that captures all of the relevant information in order to process the order. It must include:

- Your label's details, including who has taken the order
- The customer's details, including any tax numbers and billing address
- Date
- Order number
- A description of each style
- Quantity of each style, colourways, sizes and price
- Delivery address
- Delivery date.

The delivery date is the date the goods will leave you, not the date they will arrive with the customer. While you can be confident about when the goods will be packed and ready for shipping at your studio, you don't know how long a courier or shipper is going to take (you don't want to be responsible for any unforeseen shipping delays). Unless you have agreed a 'landed' selling price (whereby the cost of each unit sold includes delivery to the customer's door), the delivery and shipping costs and arrangements will be carried by the customer (see page 114 for a list of shipping terminology). It is quite common for designers to give the stores a delivery window in which the goods will arrive. This allows you to prioritise certain styles in your production run that you feel should be in the stores first or that your key stockists have ordered.

Typical Delivery Dates for Seasonal Collections (Northern Hemisphere)

Menswear autumn/winter	August
Womenswear autumn/winter	August and September
Menswear spring/summer	January
Womenswear spring/summer	Late January through to February

Christian Audigier has been able to create his lifestyle brand Ed Hardy by agreeing a licensing deal for the rights to tattoo artist Don Ed Hardy's artwork

You will also need to let buyers know when you will be closing your order books for the season – they may want to make some changes or think about numbers before signing.

Either have duplicate forms made up or print off two copies and keep one copy, giving the other to the buyer for reference.

Terms and conditions

It is imperative that you include the terms and conditions of sale on the back of your order form. This lets the buyers know exactly what they are agreeing to when signing the form. Have your solicitor look over any terms and conditions you set out to make sure you are covering yourself fully.

New customer form

It is good practice to ask new customers to fill out a new customer form, especially if they are looking for credit.

Confirmation

This is the final contract between you and the store before you go into production. This is also the time that you can invoice for your deposit if this has been agreed to. Never go into production before the confirmation is signed.

Once you have closed your order books you will need to work out your production run for the season. This means looking to see if there are any styles or colourways that you have not sold enough of to go into production. Before you send out the confirmation to the buyer, call and explain the situation. You want to be able to produce everything that has been ordered, but this is not always possible – especially in the early days when sales volume may be low.

Payment terms

It is up to you to establish payment terms with each of your customers. There are several options open to you (terminology can differ depending on the country you are selling to).

- ***Deposit:*** Ideally you would like to receive a deposit on the order when the confirmation has been signed. Anything from 25 to 50 per cent would be the norm. This should cover the costs of the goods produced if the store reneges on its order. It is more common to receive deposits from new customers for the first couple of seasons, and it is almost impossible to get deposits from the big department stores.
- ***Pre-payment:*** You can ask for the balance to be pre-paid before the goods are sent for delivery. This will help with your cash flow. It is also a good way of getting stores to pay promptly, as any delay in payment means they have empty rails and lose valuable selling time.
- ***COD (Cash on Delivery):*** This is the reverse of the pre-payment option. You send the goods to the customer who pays on receipt. If you are unfamiliar with a store ask for a money order or a direct bank transfer. (Ask your bank which payment methods will cost you less. Online banking is often cheaper.)
- ***NET Terms:*** This is where you give a period of credit before payment is due. NET 30, which is a very standard payment term, gives the customer 30 days from the date of the invoice to pay. You can ask for a deposit upfront and then the remainder of the balance NET 30. Payment terms can vary from country to country – Italy will commonly ask for NET 60 or NET 90, which can mean waiting two to three months for payment. For most new fashion start-ups terms like these will be very difficult, as cash flow is so

important to the survival of the business. Larger department stores will often dictate their payment terms, often taking a three to five per cent discount if they pay within the agreed time period. You will have to decide whether or not you can live with the loss of revenue and how important the store is to you in terms of profile-raising and turnover.

✖ **Letter of credit:** The store establishes credit with a local bank, clearly describing the goods to be purchased, the price, the documentation required, and a time limit for completion of the transaction. On receipt of the letter of credit you release the goods to the store. Most stores are reluctant to pay by this method, as it is expensive to set up.

✖ **Credit card:** For smaller stores this can sometimes be a welcome alternative, if you have the facility. You will need to factor in the charge the credit card companies will deduct from all payments made, typically anywhere between one and five per cent.

Smaller labels often have a number of different payment options with their customers, many of whom are small retailers. The more you work with a store the more they will trust you and the better the terms you might then offer them.

COMPANY LOGO

Order Form
Company Contact Details

Order No:

Order Taken By:

VAT No:

Contact Name:
Co. Name:
Date:
Address:
Tel:
Fax:
Mobile:
Email Address:
Payment Terms:
Shipping Details:
Delivery Address:
Delivery Date:

Style No.	Description	Colour/Print	XS 8	S 10	M 12	L 12	Qty	Unit Cost (£)	Total Cost (£)

Comments:

NET TOTAL

VAT

TOTAL

The supply of the garments stated here are made subject to the conditions set out on the reverse hereof, acknowledgement of which is evidenced by the signature of the Purchaser.

Signature:

Date:

To receive payment you will need to invoice your customers. Invoices must include your:

✖ Business name
✖ Trading name
✖ Logo
✖ Address and contact details
✖ Date
✖ Tax numbers (including VAT)
✖ Invoice number

and your customer's:

✖ Company name
✖ Trading name
✖ Address and contact details
✖ Date
✖ Tax numbers (including VAT)
✖ Item reference
✖ Item detail
✖ Price/item
✖ Total price
✖ Applicable tax per item
✖ Total price per item
✖ Total price, total tax
✖ Amount payable.

They should also detail your payment methods, including your bank account number, or 'cheque payable to', payment terms and status of payment. Check with your accountant to make sure you have everything required by law.

COMPANY LOGO		**Invoice**	
COMPANY NAME		Invoice No:	
COMPANY ADDRESS		Date:	

CUSTOMER

Customers Name

Customers Address

STYLE NO	NAME	MAIN FABRIC	XS	S	M	L	Qty	Unit Price £	Total Price £

	Sub Total	
	VAT	
	Delivery	
	TOTAL	

PAYMENT TERMS

BANK DETAILS FOR PAYMENT

COMPANY NO:	VAT NO:

Retailing

Harrods, one of the world's most renowned retailers, is an example of a classic department store

The biggest advantage of retailing your own product is the obvious opportunity to make bigger profit margins. There are other advantages, depending on what type of retail method you choose.

Your Own Store

Having your own shop is something all designers aspire to, and it can help with the wholesale side of your business as well. It offers buyers an opportunity to see your complete brand concept under one roof and also gives them confidence that you have a sellable product. The high risk and cost involved, however, usually means that fashion start-ups stay away from this option until they are established.

Although most fashion retailers start up as one-off small boutiques, the different types of retailers include department stores, speciality stores, boutiques, chain stores and discount stores.

The type of retailer you will aim to be will be determined by your retail theory. This will depend on your product, your ideal customer and the potential size of your shop. Your options are:

1 **Low mark-up with high volume and huge selection** (high-street mass market retailer).
2 **Higher mark-up with lower volume but with full selection** (department store).
3 **High mark-up with low volume and smaller selection** (boutique).

Now think about location (see page 76).

Internet

This continues to be a very fast-growing sector. Accessories labels do well because sizing is less of an issue for the consumer and there are few problems with returns. The relatively low overheads can mean better profit margins. The major challenge is getting people on to your site. What you save on shop rental might have to be spent on marketing.

Young fashion labels that do not have the resources to run their own e-boutique can trade through e-commerce sites such as FashionPublic, where you choose which items to sell and set the retail price. They promote your brand and provide you with exposure to new customers globally. You get all the tools you need to create your collection and sell online. When a customer places an order, they alert you immediately, and a courier collects and delivers. After the sale they deduct a sales commission and transfer funds to you.

Markets

Choosing the right market says a lot about your business. The higher in price you go the more this becomes a concern. You need to make sure the market you are selling from has a reputation for supporting designer labels.

Private Clients

Many labels start off making one-off pieces or a small sample range that they are then able to offer clients in their exact measurements. The bonus of this is that you can ask for payments to be made in stages, the first of which (deposit) should be enough to cover the cost of making. This means your initial outlay is covered. Private clients can come to you, or you can go to them. This service works well for people who are cash-rich but time-poor.

Consumer Shows

Consumer events usually take place over a short period and you will be charged for taking up a stall at the event. Ally Ward from yoga clothing collection KokoFlow says, 'Before the show I had called around everyone who exhibited there the year before so I knew what to expect, and the most useful advice was to not go overboard on spending. I kept costs low and made a simple, bright, eye-catching stand. I went with the idea in mind that what I wanted most was feedback. I found it invaluable talking to customers, buyers and even other sellers. I got loads of information, contacts and had a total blast. As a

bonus I made some sales, but not being hung up on that at my first show made everything so much better.'

Television

Home shopping networks such as QVC and the Home Shopping Channel offer a huge client base for the right fashion labels and can deliver a great deal of business if the product is right.

House Parties

Home shopping parties have moved on a long way since the early Tupperware parties and can prove a viable option for selling your product directly to your customer. Even major fashion retailers like Topshop are getting in on the act with their 'Topshop to Go' service which they advertise as 'a mobile style service aiming to provide the ultimate in home shopping'.

Trunk Shows

This could involve taking a room in a hotel in a major city where you know your collection will be well received, going to corporate businesses who want to offer their employees something unique during their lunch break, or setting up at a country club to offer members a special chance to meet the designer and buy the product direct. Some department stores also offer the opportunity for up-and-coming labels to hold trunk shows in their stores.

Yoga-inspired fashion label KokoFlow used The Yoga Show (a consumer trade show) to launch the label and gain invaluable feedback from suitable customers

Sample Sales

Taking part in sample sales throughout the year (if you have the stock) can be a great way of bringing income into your business on a regular basis. You need to be careful about selling current stock (unless faulty) at these sales, as this can undermine your stockists and will also diminish the value of your brand. The e-commerce site *www.koodos.com* gives designers the opportunity to sell samples and excess stock online.

Case Study: Karen Walker

Karen Walker set up her company, Karen Walker Limited, in 1989 when she was 19 and still at fashion college. She started with NZ$100 (US$78) of her own money and designed and made a shirt which she sold in a local boutique. The reason she started on her own was because '...there was no one around whose work I liked and who I wanted to work with'.

The company has grown rapidly into a very successful global operation. Within four years they had their first stand-alone womenswear store, opening a second one in 1994. In 1995 they started to export into markets beyond New Zealand and, by 1998, they had stockists all over the world. In 2001 they expanded beyond fashion design and started their first interior line – Karen Walker Paints – in partnership with leading paint manufacturer, Resene. They have continued to expand their product range, launching a jewellery range in 2003 and a range of eyewear in 2005.

Karen is very clear about her market and about whom she likes to work with – 'people like us'. 'We've never really worked based on location but based on personalities and as such we've developed a global niche brand. Our girl in Tokyo is the same as our girl in New York or Sydney or London.' Karen has surrounded herself with people she likes and admires and this seems to be core to her success.

To add to this, Karen also attributes her success to making products that people like and to which they can relate. Next to product, she believes that placement is key, 'because the environment tells so much about you and where you sit in the market'. Initially the business was built entirely around wholesale, but now she has her own retail stores. These are boutique shops designed to create a relaxed, stylish, intimate and fun shopping experience with lots to take in. She also licenses product, again subscribing to the 'people like us' rule. 'If we like the people and they get the idea within five minutes and have all the necessary skills and experience to make it work, and if it's a product that excited us, then we leap in.'

To keep her product in the right environment, Karen also shows at New York Fashion Week. 'It's about making it easy for your customer. Easy to see,

understand, buy. And if it's all about making it easy for your customer, you go where your customers are going to be when they're going to be there – in our case in New York during New York Fashion Week. That's not to say it's the only way though. There are lots of ways to make it easy for your customer.'

Karen places promotion and price below product and placement on the list of key contributors to success. 'PR and marketing are of course an integral part of the fashion business but I knew intuitively right from the start that unless there's substance – an actual story to tell or product worth looking at – that you could have the best PR in the world and they wouldn't be able to do anything for you. The PR you create is only ever going to be as good as the product you sell.' Price, she feels, will be set by the product, placement and promotion.

Karen is driven by the fact that she likes what she does. She says she is 'definitely still having fun, even when it's not fun. I get to structure my life how I want and I get the sense of satisfaction and pride (when it goes right) and there are a certain number of perks too.' On the downside she says that '...there's a lot of stuff that needs to be considered outside of just creating interesting design – there are a lot of distractions.' But, if you want to be successful you 'must have the ability to understand business and be creative and responsible within business. You must also be a really fast learner because it's the kind of business where you have to run or stop. No walking.'

Karen's aim is to make products that people both like and are able to relate to

Chapter 12: Get Your Message Out

Your new fashion label must convey a strong, identifiable message to which buyers, press and consumers can relate. So do you want to be seen as young, sophisticated, edgy, luxurious, affordable, accessible, unique, quirky, pretty, sexy, trendy, conservative, functional or exclusive?

Promotion is how you deliver your label's message to your target audience. It covers a wide range of activities: sales, advertising, publicity, special events and websites. Your strategy should focus on getting people to buy your product, so you must pitch your activities correctly. If you are retailing, you will need to target the end consumer. If you are wholesaling, you will target both the end consumer and the retailers.

Look at Buying Behaviour

An understanding of buying behaviour will allow you to devise promotional activities that will influence the buying process.

Typical Consumer Buying Behaviour

===

Identifies a need: *Often through press coverage, advertising, celebrity endorsement or word of mouth.*

Looks for information: *From websites, advertising and press. Can they find your label easily? Peer group recommendation is very important. Visual aids, such as catalogues, posters and so on are very useful.*

Checks out alternative suppliers and products: *Also known as 'window shopping'. You need to promote your product's uniqueness, and maximise packaging and displays. Sales personnel can have a huge influence. Make sure they are educated about your product. Third-party testimonial is still important. Value for money also becomes of major interest.*

Purchase decision: *Sales promotions and customer service come into their own.*

Use of the product: *Expensive purchases can promote cognitive dissonance (see page 95). You need to provide constant reassurance through good customer care, advertising, and third-party testimonials.*

Image by Malcolm Crews

===

Typical Business Buying Behaviour

==

Identifies a need or problem: *Usually highlighted by advertising or press coverage (trade and consumer).*

Develops product specification: *Particular attention is paid to press releases, exhibitions, advertising, editorial comment and relevant direct mail.*

Looks for products and suppliers: *Marketing material such as lookbooks, line sheets and websites are of particular importance. Exhibitions/showrooms are also an invaluable source of information. At this point, pricing information begins to be seriously considered.*

Evaluates suppliers and products: *This is a good time to provide your potential customer with third-party testimonials. This can include references from other stores you sell to as well as relevant press. It is also the time when customers expect to see and feel the product to assess style and quality.*

Places an order: *Personal contact will help to close the order and increase its size.*

Evaluates supplier and product performance: *The larger the financial commitment the more reassurance is needed. Continued exposure to advertising and press coverage, together with phone calls and emails, will help to justify the decision to purchase.*

Reorders: *The first order placed should be seen not as the end of the process, but as the beginning of a long-term relationship.*

==

Promotional Materials

Some of your promotional materials will be specific to press and buyers, whilst others will target the consumer directly.

Lookbooks

Lookbooks introduce your product line or new season's collection to press and buyers. Catwalk designers usually take the images for their lookbooks from catwalk photographs. They are often presented as an A5 wire-bound glossy booklet, with 30 to 60 looks from the show, one photograph to a page.

The lookbook must have clear photographs of all your key products, with reference numbers, contact details and website address. If you include a recommended retail price (RRP) for each garment as well as a description of the product you can use the lookbook as a small sales catalogue for consumers.

You could keep your printing costs down by selecting a few very strong images that give the essence of your collection and putting the rest on your website. However, busy journalists may just choose from the limited selection in your lookbook.

Lookbooks can come in varying shapes and sizes and are an essential tool for promoting your collection to press and buyers alike

Top Tips for Printing Lookbooks

==

Simon Assirati – *Managing Director, Solutions in Ink*

-- --

Images: The printer will always produce a far better lookbook when using very high resolution images.

'Fashion' printers focus on the garment rather than the model. The printer's job is to replicate the garments as closely as possible in printed format. This becomes increasingly technical when printing on different substrates of paper or board.

You can enhance the images, depending on the type of material used to print on – uncoated, coated matt, coated silk or coated gloss finishes.

Before going to print, always ensure you have a digital proof from the printer as a final safety check. The colour digital proof is 80 to 90 per cent accurate in terms of colour balance and is also good for spell-checking and image position.

Materials: The majority of lookbooks are printed on a uniform board-weight throughout, such as 300-gsm or 350-gsm. This will also keep the cost down. Ask your printer to provide you with a free 'mock-up' or unprinted dummy of your chosen lookbook.

Enhancing the lookbook further can be done by using specialist 'finishes' such as matt, silk or gloss lamination on the paper or board; foil blocking in myriad colours; or de-bossing or embossing the material to give it a raised or sunken feel for a specific logo or piece of type.

Dimensions and binding are down to personal choice as well as cost. Printing, then creasing the board into panels, then folding them into a 'pamphlet' type of finish is the most economical option in terms of cost. More flamboyant, costly lookbooks are stitched or bound like a magazine.

Quantity: Always print just enough to avoid surplus stock the following season. Printers will quote for batches of 500 or 1,000 so you can see the price variations.

==

Photography

Photography is especially important in a business like fashion where aesthetics are everything.

Developing a relationship with a photographer you trust is extremely important. Quite often you will be working to tight deadlines for shoots and you need to work with someone who can offer advice on what will work best and be most cost-effective. You may find the photographer can also help with things such as sourcing models, location, hair stylists and make-up artists.

Planning a Fashion Shoot

Rikard Osterlund – *Freelance fashion photographer (www.rikard.co.uk)*

Before you start, answer these simple questions. What is the purpose of the images? Who are they for? A lookbook (aimed at buyers) needs to show the details, prints and silhouette of your designs, whilst an ad or editorial (aimed at consumers) needs to tell a story and create an atmosphere.

The key ingredients are: great clothes, a beautiful model and a talented photographer.

Planning and preparation: *Have all your garments/designs ready (ironed and steamed), confirm with everyone in the team a few days before the shoot date, bring your inspiration, research, tear-sheets and mood-boards. Hair and make-up take on average one to three hours. Make a call-sheet (all members of the team, contact details, addresses, times and other info) and send it to everyone on the team.*

The team: *Photographer, model, location, lighting, stylist, hair stylist, make-up artist, props and so on. Get your team together before you finalise your idea – they are the specialists.*

Photographer: *Find the one who can best illustrate your collection. Start by looking at photographers' portfolios – the AOP is a good place to start (www.image-folio.com), or find individual websites.*

Photography plays a very important role in the promotion of your collections. It is essential that you work with photographers who understand the message you are looking to achieve for your label and who can offer you the best possible shots to represent your product

Look for one who is appropriate to your brand and collection (an amazing product photographer is perhaps not the ideal fashion photographer). Ask to meet up and have a look through the portfolio (every experienced photographer will have one). On the shoot the photographer is often the creative director so you need a good personal vibe.

Charges/fees: *There is no set rate for commercial photography. A photographer's fee varies depending on the use of the images:*

✖ *Where the images will be displayed (packaging, website)*
✖ *How long they will be displayed for (a longer licence will have a higher fee)*
✖ *Territory (UK, US, etc.).*

Licence to use/copyright: *The copyright in photographs always resides with the photographer.*

Story: *Contemporary fashion photography is more about the photograph than about the clothes. A series of images represents the dreams and desires of your clients, and it is driven by lighting, pose and story. The series of images allows you to develop characters and introduce the clothes.*

Model: *Make sure a model's features match your collection. Contact the agencies beforehand, check prices and available models – the best ones are unlikely to do jobs on a small budget, so make sure you cast them, meet them and see them in your clothes before you make the decision (that way you can check fittings). When you see a model wearing your clothes well it will click immediately.*

Book a second option in case of a no-show. Brief your model on the kind of person she or he is to become in the shoot (refer to your story).

The model's fee is based on similar parameters as the photographer's fee.

Ensure that the model signs a model release form, allowing you to use the images for your particular purpose. This is the contract (if you abuse this arrangement and hire a model for a lookbook, but use the images for a campaign, you must inform the agent and pay the additional fees).

Location:

✖ *Natural light – realistic, soft*
✖ *Flash-lighting – sculptural, fantasy*
✖ *Light is the most important element, so make sure any indoor locations have big windows*
✖ *Use your contacts here – owners of many good locations know they are good and will charge you (try to avoid doing a trade for images, because if the location uses the images for promotion it is you and your photographer who will get in trouble)*
✖ *Props – find the right props to set off your collection.*

Hair stylist and make-up artist: *These should add to your story, and the character of the model. Arrange a meeting, view portfolios and see if they are confident about working on your shoot.*

After the shoot: *Some digital photographers will give the client a CD with preview images directly after the shoot, whilst others may post a selection of images on a website. Once the images have been selected, they will be taken through the digital workflow (digital version of film-processing). Any professional fashion images are then retouched. Retouching is expensive so make sure you have limited your selection.*

Make sure you tell the photographer what you need the images for (website or posters, etc.) as the images will be set up differently depending on the output.

Line Sheets

A line sheet is a sales sheet used for wholesale purposes, providing information on all products or seasonal styles. It is usually sent out to buyers with the lookbook. It should include:

✖ Logo
✖ Season (autumn/winter; spring/summer)
✖ Styles (usually line drawings but sometimes photographs)
✖ Style names
✖ Style numbers
✖ Colour and fabric information.

On the back page include:
✖ Delivery dates and order cut-off dates
✖ Order minimums
✖ Sales agent's contact information.

Additional information:
✖ Swatch card.

STORY	STYLE NAME	STYLE NO.	COLOUR NAME	UPPER	UK W/S (X 2.6)	UK RRP	IMAGE
Figure of eight	TABITHA	LG2447	Black	Patent leather	£75.00	£195.00	
Figure of eight	TESSA	LG2461	Plum	Leather	£71.15	£185.00	
Figure of eight	RENE	LG2444	Black stripes Raspberry black	Textile	£75.00	£195.00	
Figure of eight	SUNNY	LG2442	Black Raspberry	Patent leather	£67.50	£175.00	
Figure of eight	ISABELLA	LG2420	Plum	Leather	£61.55	£160.00	
Figure of eight	ISABELLA	LG2421	Black stripes	Textile	£61.55	£160.00	
Figure of eight	FIFI	LG2438	Plum Black Cream	Patent leather	£65.50	£170.00	
Figure of eight	FIFI	LG2439	Bronze	Leather	£65.50	£170.00	
Figure of eight	FIFI	LG2478	Raspberry	Suede	£65.50	£170.00	
Figure of eight	FREDERICA	LG2449	Plum Bronze Raspberry	Leather	£52.00	£135.00	
Figure of eight	FREDERICA	LG2450	Black Cream	Patent leather	£52.00	£135.00	

Line sheets are used for sales purposes and provide the buyer with the key information needed to place an order

Stationery

You will need business cards, letterheads and comp slips, designed to reinforce your label's image.

Swing Tickets

Stores will expect you to attach swing tickets to your products for retail purposes. It can also look professional to have swing tickets (with the wholesale price) when wholesaling.

Labels

The customer looks to the label of a garment to identify the brand and gauge the quality of the product. You can have your label custom-made by a manufacturer to make it unique.

You will also need care labels. These should include fabric information, care advice and other special instructions. They communicate the size of the garment and the place of origin (laws on place of origin details vary from country to country).

When developing your swing tickets it is important to carry through the brand image you are looking to project. Iconic Japanese streetwear label Bathing Ape has cleverly incorporated its logo into a camouflage design to reinforce its brand message

Websites

Much as a shop window should entice a customer into the store, your website should entice people into your brand.

Websites are often the first point of contact for press, buyers and consumers looking for information on your label and therefore need to project your message clearly.

Top Tips for Planning a Website

==

1   *Select a colour scheme and stick to it.*

2   *Templates can be a cheap and effective way of developing your site (see www.web4business.com.au; www.templates.bigwebmaster.com/ fashion/; www.webuildpages.com/web-design/fashion-website-templates. htm; www.website-templates-resale-rights.com; www.templatemonster.com; www.templatesbox.com.)*

3   *Make navigation around the site as easy as possible.*

4   *Don't get carried away with special effects.*

5   *Make sure fonts can be easily read against backgrounds.*

6   *Content is king.*

==

Events

Exhibitions
Exhibitions are a great place to meet trade and consumer press and promote your name and brand, so have a press pack (see page 152) available. Consumer shows also give your label direct exposure to the public.

Networking Events
People, especially the right people, need to know about you. Official networking events for small business owners and the fashion industry take place all the time so keep an eye out for any press announcements of such events.

Getting out and about to parties is also a great way of spreading your name around. Getting invited to the right parties where the fashionistas hang out is all about befriending the event organisers. The greater your label's reputation, the more invites you will receive.

Catwalks are often an exciting way for fashion labels to promote their latest collections and, depending on the market you are looking to target, may take place either during the major fashion weeks around the world or at consumer shows direct to the public

Catwalks
The catwalk is the designer's one opportunity each season to invite the world's press and buyers to see the latest creations and gain as much exposure as possible.

Catwalk Checklist

==

Venue
Is the venue large enough, centrally located and visually suitable for your brand? Can it accommodate a catwalk, seating for guests and a large backstage area?

Risk assessment/insurance
You will need to check that the venue has public liability insurance. If producing the show yourself you will need public liability and employer liability insurance.

Catwalk/runway
A raised catwalk allows a large audience to get a good look at the collection from the top of the model's head to the shoes on her feet. A floor-level runway area can work just as well.

Music
The music you choose should help create the story your collection is trying to tell the audience. You will need a performing rights licence. If you're using a DJ, check with him/her to see if they have a licence. If not, you'll need to apply for a one-day permit.

Personnel
Backstage you will need a team of dressers. Students from fashion colleges are happy to help out in this capacity. They must be briefed individually on the outfits they are in charge of – any detailing of position or placement needs to be explained.

Try to have someone to look after front-of-house, including guests.

Models
Use reputable model agencies. The number and reputation of your models will depend on the size of your budget. You will need to hold a casting – look through the models' portfolios and get them to walk up and down to make sure they are suitable for the look of your show. Don't take too much time with each. Take a picture of those you like in order to remember them. Once you have made your selection call the agencies to book the models. If there are a number of shows on at the same time they will give you an option. As the show gets closer they will confirm. You will need to give a call time for the models to arrive on the day. It is quite common during a busy period to have only four hours before the show – other shows may run late and so will your models. Make sure there are refreshments for the models – you want them to look and feel their best.

You must negotiate with the agency for usage. Most fees only include the catwalk show; if you want to use images from the show for lookbooks, websites or advertising, you will need to pay more.

Photographer
Book a catwalk photographer to take photos to send out to press contacts who didn't manage to come along. Try to get one with good press contacts and who has experience of taking catwalk pictures. See www.vogue.com or www.style.com for the type of shots you should be looking for.

Lighting
Get professional help. It needn't be expensive but you need to have the right lighting for the photography.

Hair and make-up
You will need a dedicated hair and make-up team. They might need 30 to 60 minutes per model. Fashion colleges or hair salons can be a good place to find people to work for nothing – as long as they get a mention. You may be able to get sponsorship (see below).

Invitations
These should be sent out at least four weeks in advance of your catwalk show (less if you are showing during an official fashion week and your name has been put on a schedule). Invitations should be ready to go to print at least six weeks in advance. Do a call-around closer to the show to gauge numbers and start to devise a seating plan. It is common to see press seated on one side and buyers, celebrities and VIPs on the other.

Compère
If you are organising a catwalk show for consumers to watch rather than trade buyers and press it can be a good idea to have a compère introducing the show – someone with confidence and a good sense of humour. You may want to produce a script to make sure all the sponsors get a mention and the important points about your collection are put across.

Credit sheet and press release
A credit sheet with acknowledgements, sponsors' logos and an at-show press release (with your contact details) about the collection should be placed on each seat.

Press and media
A month before the show, send out a press release and follow up with a phone call. Two weeks beforehand send out another press release and follow up with another phone call. You will need to give the press an angle. Catwalk shows are great visual stories and can generate regional and national TV coverage.

===

Press Days

Labels that don't show on the catwalk often arrange a day for the press to come and view the collection in person in a hotel in a central location, or in the designer's studio. As an unknown label you will need to work hard to make sure the press attend – you may find that taking the collection to the press is more effective in the early days.

Sponsorship/Collaborations

Sponsorship of catwalk shows is very common. Beauty and lifestyle giants such as L'Oréal will often get involved with the hair and make-up and can send out the message that you are working with some of the industry's biggest and best brands.

Brands like Mizani look to work with designers and shows that complement their own brand ethos and promote their products to a wider audience

Nzinga Russell for Mizani says:

'Mizani is a premium haircare range specifically formulated for the hair and scalp of excessively curly hair textures. As an exclusive, salon-only, professional brand we are committed to the stylist and part of this commitment is our passion for fashion and creativity. This is why Kulture 2 Couture was perfect for us.

'As a growing brand we are always looking for opportunities to raise our profile as well as inspire creativity. K2C fulfilled both of these needs as it allowed us to strengthen our link with fashion. Supporting up-and-coming talent is often one of the most rewarding and exciting ways of doing this. It's also always good to get involved with an initiative early on in its development as you can then create real synergy and collaboration between the two brands.

'Hair and fashion are inextricably linked so not only did the relationship make great commercial sense for us, it was something we were fundamentally passionate about which made for a great pairing.'

Designers can often also be asked to take part in collaborative projects. A make-up brand may ask a designer to come up with a limited edition make-up bag. A mobile phone company may want a phone case for promotional purposes. This can be a great way for your label to gain wider recognition and a welcome source of income. Whilst it is often the marketing managers who approach the designers, don't be afraid to put a pitch together if you think you have a great idea that would tie in brilliantly with another company's marketing strategy.

Caroline Mackay, Brand Manager for Knomo:

'As a new tech-relevant accessories brand, we wanted to up the ante in the fashion stakes and really make a splash with the fashion press. We were put in touch with fashion event OnlOff and came across the beautiful designs of fashion label Belle & Bunty. Together we hit upon the idea of putting one of

their striking prints across our best-selling "Cholet" women's bag. We certainly got what we hoped for – the bags were a huge hit with customers and were featured in *Marie Claire* and *Grazia*; we were only sorry we didn't produce more of them!'

Public Relations

PR is crucial in getting your fashion label's message out and is a much more cost-effective medium than advertising. It is well suited to the fashion industry because there is always something new to write about.

What's Your Story?

You need to understand what it is the fashion press want to cover. Examine how and why magazines put together the fashion pages as they do.

Niki Turner, PR and Marketing Manager for Kurt Geiger:

'Understand the publication you are pitching to. Ensure you demonstrate knowledge of their pages and don't ever just do a blanket pitch for a story. Find an angle to suit each publication and always make sure you only get in contact with a story that is relevant and will be of interest. Remember, a journalist receives hundreds of press releases a week so be imaginative and work out the best approach to get their attention without being detrimental to your brand. The most common complaint I hear from fashion journalists is the amount of rubbish they get sent through with no forethought into what their page/column is about. Journalists are keen to hear about stories that have a hook and are newsworthy such as collaborations, charity link-ups and celebrity.'

Top Tips for Getting Press Coverage

==

✖ **Play reporter:** *Think like the journalist. What is it they want to cover for their readership? What topics or products are of interest? What angles will they find fresh and provocative?*

✖ **Tailored pitches:** *When you deliver a pitch, you're tailoring an idea for a single reporter. You're saying, 'I think you'll be interested in this idea because...'.*

✖ **Think long term:** *Get to know the journalists so that even if the reporter doesn't take you up on your offer this time, you can be confident your next pitch will be read. It's all about relationships.*

==

Press Pack

When approaching the media you should have a press pack containing all the material needed to cover your story. A basic pack should include:

✖ History and overview
✖ Designer's biography
✖ Lookbook
✖ Press release
✖ Contact details.

The label's history and the designer's biography will need constant updating, while your lookbook will need to be reprinted seasonally to reflect your new product range. Journalists and stylists will go through the lookbooks for key pieces to shoot for their publication.

Press releases should be tailored to the specific story or announcement. Typical stories that might warrant a release include: launch of your new collection, new major distribution outlets for your product, celebrity tie-ins.

Format for a Typical Press Release

==

FOR IMMEDIATE RELEASE
These words should appear in the upper left-hand margin with all letters capitalised.

Headline
A sentence that gives the essence of what the press release is about. Articles, prepositions and conjunctions of three-letter words or fewer should be lowercase.

Dateline
The city from which your press release is issued and the date you are mailing your release.

Lead paragraph
A strong introductory paragraph should grab the reader's attention and should contain the information most relevant to your message, such as the five W's (who,

what, when, where, why). It should summarise the press release and include a hook to get your audience interested in reading more.

Body
This is where your message should fully develop. Many companies choose to use a strategy called the inverted pyramid, which is written with the most important information and quotes first.

Boilerplate
Your press release should end with a short paragraph that describes your label, products, service and a short history.

Contact details
Name, phone number, email address and website.

===

Your press pack will not guarantee coverage. PR is about developing relationships with the media, and you will need to pick up the phone and talk directly with the journalists responsible for the particular column you are looking to get into. When you call you need to know exactly what you are going to say and that you are talking to the right person. Once the relationship has been established you will find that journalists start coming to you with call-ins (see below) for shoots and editorials. This is when you know the relationship is working.

===

TASK

Draw up a hotlist of 20 journalists or editors
Identify the publications whose readerships best match your target customer. Go through each publication and make a list of the key journalists and the pages they are responsible for. Narrow them down to the key 20 journalists. These will be the focus of your PR activities.

===

Call-Ins
A call-in is when a journalist or stylist requests your product for a still life or editorial shoot they are doing. They will usually say they are interested in particular pieces of your collection that they have seen in your lookbook. If you have only a few images in your lookbook this could be the time to point them in the direction of extra images on your website. The more they choose, the greater the likelihood there is of something being shot for their story.

Responsibility for getting your product to the journalist or stylist can differ depending on the publication or programme calling in the pieces. Major publications and TV shows will often arrange for a courier at their expense. They will also be responsible for the return delivery. This obviously depends on whether you are located near the major media outlets. At other times you may be responsible for delivering your collection. Don't be afraid to ask if they can arrange for a pick-up. If you are based away from the main media outlets, you may need to look for representation with a PR agency based close to the key publications. They will hold on to your most pressworthy samples for call-ins and will take over the responsibility of all your press enquiries.

Keeping track

Once a call-in has come through make a record of exactly what is being sent out, when and to whom, and the shoot date. Keep one copy and put one in the package (with your contact details) with the call-in. Include a disclaimer that all damaged or unreturned pieces will be charged at full price. The press can call in hundreds of pieces a day, all of which will go through their fashion cupboard, and things can go astray. You want to get your pieces back as soon as they have been shot to make sure you are ready for the next time they are called in.

Press Book and Show Cards

Just because your product gets called in doesn't mean it will actually make the final publication or programme. If your product is being featured in a magazine, you will usually receive a phone call requesting a recommended retail price and a stockist's address or phone number. Once you know your product has been covered find out which edition it will be featured in. Buy a copy to add to your press book. It is a great tool for showing buyers, consumers and potential investors about the buzz your label is creating. You can also put press coverage on your website.

Show cards are a great way of letting buyers and customers know the press you have achieved and can help to sell your product

For really great pieces of press, you can order show cards from the publication, for a fee. Feature your show cards prominently at trade exhibitions to show potential buyers that you are a label that is being talked about. You can also get a few extra cards for any key stockists that have bought the piece featured to display.

Dressing Celebrities

Getting your product endorsed by the right celebrity can do wonders for your fashion label. However, the message you send is irretrievably linked with the message the celebrity sends out. If you are producing expensive red-carpet dresses this can be great if the celebrity is a suave and sophisticated Hollywood A-lister, but not so great if the celebrity is regarded as a cheap and tacky D-lister.

The key to dressing celebrities is building a relationship with their stylists. Although the celebrity will ultimately choose what they think suits them best they can be heavily influenced by their stylists. The more visible your fashion label, the more likely it is that a fashion stylist will contact you to request product. However, services such as Red Pages (*www.theredpages.co.uk*) offer access to contact details for celebrities all over the world for a monthly fee. Quite often the contact is the agent representing the celebrity. It is then up to you to contact them. Usually they will write back and point you in the direction of the stylist.

Oz and Kat Aalam from London boutique Damsel say:

'The most helpful thing to us from a selling point of view is magazine features or celebrity coverage.'

In House v Agency

If the thought of cold calling journalists turns you into a quivering wreck it then may be best to find someone to do your PR, either in house or through a reputable agency specialising in fashion PR.

Pros and Cons

==

In House

Advantages:

- ✘ Has onsite access to other key internal functions
- ✘ Can deal quickly and effectively with range of external queries
- ✘ Understands the brand's market position/history in depth
- ✘ Gives 100 per cent effort and attention to your label.

Disadvantage:

- ✘ Is a fixed cost to your business (although can be part-time).

Agency

Advantages:

- ✘ Specialist team with resources (writers and production)
- ✘ Objectivity may produce fresh ideas and approach
- ✘ Wider range of contacts/experience
- ✘ Variable cost to your business.

Disadvantage:

- ✘ Focus may be on bigger clients.

==

PR agencies usually work on a monthly retainer basis and costs can vary from £500 a month for a small agency taking on a start-up to £10,000+ for the top agencies working with more established brands. If you are working to a very tight budget, spend on sales rather than a PR agency, which is a long-term investment. There are hundreds of fashion labels in existence that you will never have heard of, as they do not have a high media profile, but are making very nice money for themselves. They have focused on developing a strong customer base through marketing and sales activities rather than chasing the press. All the hype in the world won't make your business a success if your product disappoints your customers.

Chapter 13: Finance

*T*he financial side of setting up a fashion label is quite often the area that most aspiring fashion entrepreneurs decide to tackle last. However, it's better to sort out the financial aspects of your business right from the outset. As Caroline Charles states: 'Try not to separate the design and marketing process from the finance side – the sooner you can embrace them all as part of the creative process the greater success and more fun you will have.' This chapter will take you through the steps you need to take to get your business off the ground and raise it to a sustainable level. This will include the cost of office space, manufacturing, marketing, office equipment and contingency.

Projecting Your Start-Up Costs

The Converse stand at trade show Bread & Butter

Projecting your start-up costs often proves tricky for new fashion labels. The box below shows the main initial expenses and ongoing expenses that you will typically encounter. By researching the areas listed you should be able to come up with a good estimate for each area. Include your reasonable salary expectations even if at first you will be unable to draw a salary. With only a limited pot of money available you must prioritise your costs.

Start-Up Costs

Initial Expenses	Ongoing Expenses
Incorporating	Rent or mortgage
Legal and accounting	Utilities
Office/studio costs including: rent, security deposit or property purchase, furniture, equipment	Staff payroll/your salary
Research including: production, fabric/trim suppliers, exhibitions, customer base	Production
Travel	Marketing/sales/advertising
Marketing materials: business cards, letterheads, websites, etc	Travel
First samples	Insurance
	Taxes
	Debt repayment
	Working capital

Projecting the Monies You'll Make

Projecting income can be much harder than projecting costs. Most fashion start-ups will not have a starting point from which to predict turnover. You will have to make assumptions based on research into your given market. After your first 12 months of trading you will at least have the previous year's figures to go on.

Start by predicting the number of shops you aim to sell to in your first season. Initial orders from boutiques might range from just £1,000 to £2,000 – the buyers will want to see how well you will sell. If you aim to sell to high-street retailers you may find that you can sell significantly larger numbers, ranging from the hundreds to thousands per unit, with one account producing tens of thousands of pounds in income.

When projecting income in the early stages, look at your projected income and ask 'What if?' What if you only make half the sales you have projected? What if you only make a quarter? What if you make no first season sales? These are the scenarios that might drastically affect your business from the very outset.

Although your personal finances may cover most of your start-up costs, you might need a cash injection to pay for production in your first season. By having pinpointed your shortfall early, you will be in a position to start a dialogue with your bank in time for an overdraft to be in place as and when needed.

Check Out Sources of Funding

Thoroughly research the finance available to you and make sure you understand the terms and conditions of any loan. Have your accountant look over the possibilities, which might include:

✖ Personal savings
✖ Friends and relatives
✖ Banks and credit unions
✖ Grants
✖ Business angels/venture capital firms.

Personal Savings

If the amount needed to set up the label is relatively small, you may be able to cover it from your personal finances. You retain control by not relying on hand-outs from others who may want to have some say in the running of things. The obvious downside is that it's your money you're risking!

Friends and Relatives

Borrowing money from friends and relatives is quite often an emotional choice and can put a strain on relationships if the lending terms are not laid out in full or adhered to. Write down the terms under which the money is being lent, and when and under what circumstances repayment is due.

Banks and Building Societies

High-street banks and building societies will provide a loan or an overdraft if you can show that your business proposal is sound. However, quite often the decisions are generated by computers, which will use your current status to assess the risk.

Ideally loans should be used for paying for assets, such as sewing machines and computers, for start-up capital and for other cases where the amount of money you need is fixed. It is quite common for a loan guarantee to be required.

An overdraft is often used to help your business with its day-to-day cash flow, including working capital, and ongoing expenses. Expenses are best funded from the cash received from your sales, but where a shortfall may arise in the short term it is possible to use an overdraft as back-up.

Check out any lender with the Financial Services Authority (FSA). Compare lending rates and security requirements on *www.moneysupermarket.com* or *www.moneyexpert.com*.

Remember:

Most lenders will require you to:
- ✖ *Match their loan from your own resources*
- ✖ *Have a fall-back option if it all goes wrong*
- ✖ *Offer something as security – you should take professional advice before entering a secured loan agreement*
- ✖ *Keep them regularly informed of your progress, particularly any changes or problems*
- ✖ *Have a comprehensive business plan.*

Grants

Grants are given to businesses or individuals for a specified purpose or project. As long as you stick to any conditions stipulated by the grant, you will not have to repay it or give up shares in your business. However, grants usually cover only part of the total costs – it is common for you to have to match funds. Grants that apply to your specific needs can take a lot of research to find and even more paperwork to achieve. Just make sure that the time spent trying to obtain the grant isn't costing your business more than the amount of the grant.

The Business Link for London website (*www.businesslink.org.uk*) offers a search facility for grants and support schemes from central and local governments and private organisations.

Business Angels and Venture Capital Firms

Business angels are wealthy private investors who take equity stakes in small, high-risk firms.

They will often provide their own business expertise to make sure their investment has the best chance of success. Although more likely to invest in a business that has a successful track record, some prefer to spread their wealth in smaller investment amounts to young entrepreneurs with a great business plan. Small fashion start-ups often find their angels through word of mouth and introductions from friends and family. The British Business Angels Association offers advice and tips (*www.bbaa.org.uk*).

On a much larger scale (investments of £1m upwards), venture capital firms usually help expanding businesses grow in exchange for equity or partial ownership. The fashion industry is a bad risk for venture capital as it is not considered to have high or fast returns.

Once you have decided on the right route you must draw up a financial plan that will make sense to both you and your prospective lender.

Make an Offer that Can't Be Refused

Your business plan must be succinct and explain as clearly as possible exactly what you intend to do. It should outline the nature and type of your business, any personal investment and how that will be used to meet specific goals, timelines, financial objectives, analysis of your competition and how your business will fit in the marketplace. It should be watertight and convince prospective lenders that you and your business are a good investment. There are many organisations that you can go to for advice with writing your business plan and your local Business Link should be able to point you in the right direction. Ask if they know of anyone with specialist knowledge of the fashion industry.

Elements of a Business Plan

===

1 Cover sheet

2 Statement of purpose

3 Table of contents

I. The business
✖ *Description of business*
✖ *Marketing*
✖ *Competition*
✖ *Operating procedures*
✖ *Personnel*
✖ *Business insurance*
✖ *SWOT analysis*

II. Financial data
✖ *Loan applications*
✖ *Capital equipment and supply list*
✖ *Balance sheet*
✖ *Break-even analysis*
✖ *Profit and loss statements – detail by month, for first three years (include assumptions upon which projections were based – inflation, growth, currency rates, if applicable)*
✖ *Month-by-month cash flow*

III. Supporting documents
✖ *Tax returns of principals for last three years*
✖ *Personal financial statement (all banks have these forms)*
✖ *Copy of proposed lease or purchase agreement for building space*
✖ *Copies of licences and other legal documents*
✖ *Copies of CVs of all principals*
✖ *Copies of letters of intent from suppliers, etc.*

===

Top Tips for Preparing a Business Plan

===

✖ *Research (use search engines) to find business plan templates on the internet.*
✖ *Spell out strategies on how you intend to handle adversities.*
✖ *Spell out the strengths and weaknesses of your management team.*
✖ *Include at least a monthly one-year cash flow projection.*
✖ *Package your business plan in an attractive kit as a selling tool.*
✖ *Submit your business plan to experts in your intended business for their advice.*
✖ *Freely and frequently modify your business plans to account for changing conditions after start up, but always keep the original and a summary of why changes are occurring.*

===

Fill In the Gaps

Cash flow projections illustrating both the viability of your start-up and your ability to repay any loans will probably be asked for. Keep the figures realistic and back them up with facts that validate your estimates and projections. Ask your accountant to look over the numbers, but remember that you will need to be able to explain to any lenders what the figures mean and what the consequences of not hitting targets will be.

Practice Makes Perfect

In order to access start-up financing you will need to present your ideas at some point. Take time to think your pitch through and practise in front of other people who can provide constructive feedback. You need to be prepared for all kinds of questions about your business concept including product, price, market and your own personal background.

Top Tips for Pitching to Potential Investors

Excite
Express passion about your company. Try to create a buzz if you want them to remember you.

Keep it short
Stick to the basics. Don't overwhelm them with information.

Engage the audience
Encourage questions and provoke discussion by asking your own questions about the investors, their interests and past ventures.

Avoid templates
Tailor your pitch to fit the needs of your company and the investors to whom you are presenting.

Be truthful
Don't try to be more than you are or can be just to impress the investors.

Be clear, detailed and concise
Make sure that you keep the language simple and resist the urge to use jargon. Talk about your fashion business's unique points, your product, customers and what market void you are looking to fill and how you are going to fill it. Introduce your team, their relevant qualifications and the role that they will play. Outline your business model and map out your financial projections (up to five years), requirements and milestones.

Be realistic
Show that you have ambitious plans for your fashion business but don't get carried away. Investors will want to see you have a grip on the market and reality.

Be in control
Remember that investment is a two-way relationship. You are looking for the right investors as much as they are looking for the right investment. Be confident and in control.

==

Questions, Questions, Questions

Borrowing money is a big step. Get all the information you need about potential lenders' processes and loan expectations. Speak with friends and relatives about lenders they have used and involve your accountant in the process.

Find a Good Accountant

A good accountant can save you a lot of money and need not be expensive.

Use the national database compiled by the Institute of Chartered Accountants at *www.icaewfirms.co.uk*, the Chartered Institute of Management Accountants at *www.cimaglobal.com* or the Association of Chartered Certified Accountants at *www.accaglobal.com*.

How to Cost Your Product

If you're to sell at a profit, you need to have calculated the cost correctly. Although many companies are good at calculating the direct costs of things such as fabric, the other components (thread, fastening, trims, labels, freight, etc.) are often not as well costed.

Some designers simply add from 30 to 40 per cent to the final product cost to include overheads, also known as indirect costs, before adding their profit margin. While this can make costing easier it can be more difficult to cut costs.

A useful tool in calculating the true cost of your product is the Cost of Goods spreadsheet (see page 171). The headings in your spreadsheet will depend on the product you are making, but the template should give you an idea of the costs you should be factoring in. Most costs will be straightforward. Others will need to be calculated before being entered. You may pay £160 to have a dress pattern cut and graded. If you anticipate selling only one dress then you will have to factor in the full £160. However, if you believe you will sell 20, the cost per dress will be £160 ÷ 20 = £8. If you will reuse this pattern on a seasonal basis, the actual cost for each garment may be minimal.

By working through the spreadsheet you can develop wholesale and retail price points for your product. This will depend on the mark-up you decide to work from. Designer labels often mark up between two and three times, or 100 to 200 per cent. With a mark-up of three, roughly one third covers the costs, one third covers the overheads and the final third is profit.

However, many designers start by determining how much their product should be retailing for – the perceived value. If you start from this you can then divide by the standard retail mark-up to get your wholesale price. If you aim to sell a dress at a retail price of £270, and divide by what is a fairly standard UK retail mark-up of 2.7 for designer boutiques, you get a wholesale price of £100. If you then decide to work to a 2.5 mark-up from cost price to wholesale price you can work out that you need to produce the dress for a cost price of £40.

The Cost of Goods spreadsheet can help here. If the dress is costing £45 to produce you can see which components are costing too much and which design elements you will have to change. If you decide to reduce your mark-up be sure that your business can handle the loss of income.

Alternatively, if the dress is costing only £36 to produce, your mark-up to wholesale will be closer to 2.8 and your profit margin greater.

Always ask buyers what mark-up they use to get their retail price. It is often a good idea to implement an RRP to make sure your product is sold everywhere at the same price.

Mark-ups and Margins

Mark-up and margin are different ways of calculating profit, and the difference can be confusing. The mark-up is the percentage of the cost price you add to get the selling price. A 150 per cent mark-up on a product that has cost you £50 would mean a selling price of £125. This is often also expressed as a mark-up of 2.5 (125 ÷ 50 = 2.5).

A margin is the percentage of the final selling price that is profit. If you are selling a product at £150 that cost you £50 to make, your margin would be 66 per cent ([150 - 50] ÷ 150 x 100 = 66 per cent). Just remember that a selling price with a margin of 50 per cent results in more profit than a selling price with a mark-up of 50 per cent. (See box opposite.) For example, if a sweater is selling for £100 and is clearing a 50 per cent margin, it cost £50. If the same sweater had a mark-up of 50 per cent, the retail price would be £75, with £25 less profit.

Any profit you calculate in this way will be considered your *gross* profits. You will still need to deduct your overheads (rates, fixed costs, corporation tax, wages, etc.), also known as indirect costs, before you arrive at your net profit.

You may find it easier to be flexible and have a different mark-up for each product in your range. This will give you a variety of mark-ups in your product line. So, if you were selling men's and women's jeans, you might find that your women's range can tolerate a mark-up of only twice the cost (or 100 per cent), but that your men's range market can tolerate a mark-up of 3.5 times cost (or 250 per cent). Over time you will become better at reading the market value and at maximising your overall profit margins.

Top Tips for Calculating Margins

You will often have to calculate margins. Either to work out a selling price from a cost price, or to work out what margin a certain selling price would result in.

Selling price from cost price

The full formula for working out a selling price from a cost price and a certain margin is:

Selling = cost ÷ ([100 - margin] ÷ 100)

So to calculate the selling price of a pair of jeans with a 70% margin that have cost £30 to make, it would look like this: 30 ÷ ([100 - 70] ÷100) = £100

Alternatively you can simplify the calculation by using the following.

A 25% margin = cost price ÷ 0.75
A 40% margin = cost price ÷ 0.6
A 50% margin = cost price ÷ 0.5
A 70% margin = cost price ÷ 0.3

Margin from cost and selling prices

Sometimes you will have a cost and a selling price, and need to know what margin that results in. The formula is:

Margin = (1 - [cost ÷ selling]) x 100

So the calculation of the margin for jeans selling for £100 that cost £30 to make would look like this: (1 - [30 ÷ 100]) x 100 = 70%

Or to simplify you can use the following:

If cost ÷ selling is 0.25, the margin is 75%
If cost ÷ selling is 0.60, the margin is 40%
If cost ÷ selling is 0.5, the margin is 50%
If cost ÷ selling is 0.3, the margin is 70%

Gross profit

Gross profit is the difference between your sales income and the cost of making your product.

Gross profit = selling price - direct costs

If direct cost = £50 and I mark it up 2.2 I will get a selling price of £110 and my gross profit will be £60. If I then sell 1000 pieces at £110, I will make £110,000 worth of sales. However, if I subtract my original cost of £50 per garment (1000 x £50 = £50,000) then my gross profit will be £60,000.

Net profit

Net profit is the money left after subtracting all your indirect costs away from your gross profit.

Net profit = gross profit - indirect costs

If my indirect costs for example were £55,000 then my net profit from the £60,000 gross would be £5,000. Net profit is the money you would pump back into your business if you are a sole trader, or after the deduction of Corporation Tax if you are running a limited company.

Looking After the Books

While a business may be able to sustain itself for a short period without sales or profits, without cash it can't function. You must keep a close eye on your financial accounts and monitor your inflow and outflow of cash.

In order to make a profit, you will often have to deliver goods to your customers before payments are received. If you don't have enough money at your disposal to pay your suppliers and staff before your stockists pay you, you'll be unable to deliver your goods and make a profit.

To trade effectively and grow your business, you will need to build up cash reserves by ensuring that the timing of cash movements in and out of your account puts you in an overall positive cash flow situation.

Cash Flow

==

Cash is the measure of your ability to pay your bills on a regular basis.

Your cash includes: *Coins and notes, current accounts and short-term deposits, bank overdrafts and short-term loans, foreign currency and deposits that can be quickly converted to your currency.*

Your cash does not include: *Long-term deposits, long-term borrowing, money owed to suppliers (but does include any relevant interest costs), money owed by customers, stock.*

==

Cash Flow Forecasting

The cash flow forecast will typically look at the upcoming quarter or year by month and will show both the cash coming into your business, and from where, as well as the cash going out and where it will go. It will focus on receipts, payments, excess of receipts over payments – with negative figures shown in brackets, opening bank balance, closing bank balance. It is important to be realistic about your potential sales growth for the next year. One way of doing this is to take your sales revenues for the previous 12-month period and add on the percentage predicted for the next year's economic growth.

Book-keeping

By law you must keep financial records and hold on to them for a six-year period. The records you keep will need to be accurate and regularly updated, as you will have to pay a financial penalty if you cannot prove the information you have submitted for your VAT (if you are registered) or Income or Corporate Tax returns. The two most important records you need to keep will be:

1   Receipts and expenditure

2   Goods you have purchased and goods you have sold.

Tips for Effective Book-keeping

What you need to do	When (minimum timescale recommended)
Record sales in the sales ledger	At a set time every month
Record payments received in the sales ledger	At a set time every month
Record purchases in the purchase ledger	At a set time every month
Record payments made in the purchase ledger	At a set time every month
Reconcile the sales and purchase ledgers	Every month
Chase all outstanding payments	As soon as they are overdue
Check your cash book against your bank statements and your sales and purchase ledgers against your cash book	Every time you receive a bank statement

Source: *Business link* (www.businesslink.org.uk)

These days most new business owners keep their records on computer but paper records are just as valid. What's important is that they are accurate and up-to-date. If you feel that this is an area that you might struggle with, there are a number of options available to you:

1 There are software packages that will provide a framework for keeping your accounts. When you set up your business bank account you may be offered one of these. However, you might end up spending money on a product that you still don't quite understand and are unable to use. Two of the most popular are SAGE and Microsoft Office Accounting Professional. The Business Link website offers a good overview.

2 Your accountant will probably offer a book-keeping service. The better the state of the records you hand over, the less time it will take to do the books and the more money you will save. Your accountant will have software for record-keeping, so don't spend out on a software package if you don't need one.

3 Independent book-keepers. Good book-keepers can cost anywhere from £12 an hour upwards, and if your receipts are well filed you may not need them for more than a couple of hours at a time. Check local directories, shop windows and the internet for book-keepers advertising their services, or ask for a referral from another local business.

4 Many government-funded small business support organisations offer free financial record-keeping set-up services whereby they come to your premises and set up a basic book-keeping spreadsheet, giving you a brief tutorial on what information needs to be input and when. Check with your local Business Link office.

VAT (Value Added Tax)

This is a tax on the sale of goods and services levied throughout the European Union (although known by different names in different member states). The rate of tax varies from one EU member state to another; however, in the UK the standard rate is 17.5 per cent. As a business start-up you do not have to register yourself for VAT until your turnover exceeds the level stipulated by HMRC (see *www.hmrc.gov.uk*). Once you have reached the threshold, you are by law liable to register and you will have to charge VAT on your sales, keep proper VAT records on your incoming and outgoing transactions and pay HMRC. You will be expected to submit a quarterly VAT return to HMRC. Recent schemes have been set up to simplify the return process for small businesses:

Annual account scheme: Make monthly or quarterly payments based on an estimate of your total annual VAT bill. Any over/under-payment is settled at the end of the year.

Cash accounting scheme: Under this scheme you will have to pay VAT to HMRC only when your customers have paid you.

Flat rate scheme: Under this scheme VAT is calculated as a percentage of your turnover. The percentage is decided according to the trade sector your business is in.

Improving Everyday Cash Flow

For any small business cash flow can be tricky, but within the fashion industry (and especially if you are working to the two-season-a-year wholesale calendar) it can be doubly so. There are a few things you can do to try to make life easier for yourself. (And see Top Tips for Improving Your Cash Flow, overleaf.)

Ask customers to pay sooner

Most boutiques, independent shops and department stores will expect credit and will pay you after the goods have been received. This means you could be looking at only two windows a year when money will be coming into the business. To avoid this, ask for a deposit on confirmation of the order. This is usually to cover the costs of production and can cover you in case the shop goes out of business or reneges on the order mid-season. It is also worth asking for the remainder of the payment pro forma when the goods are ready to be delivered. This means the shop pays you as soon as the goods are with you and ready to go – once the monies have cleared, the goods are shipped. Even if the shop won't pay the full amount pro forma it may be worth trying to negotiate 50 per cent of the outstanding balance pro forma and giving credit (30 days is standard) for the remainder.

Use a factor

When you have sent your delivery to your stockists you send your invoices for each customer to a factor, who typically advances up to 80 or 90 per cent of the invoice amount to you. The final balance is paid to you, minus the factor's fees, when your customer makes payment directly to the factor. Your customer will receive a letter from your factor with your invoice, and payment instructions. It can take as little as 24 hours for the funds to be released to you.

The factor's fees are calculated as a service charge of 0.6–3.0 per cent of the invoiced amount, and interest charge on the cash advances. The service charge will be based on your annual turnover, number of invoices and number of customers. The interest charge is typically comparable to normal secured bank overdraft rates.

Factors will offer a range of services. Typically the most common are: recourse factoring, when the risk of bad debts remains with you; and non-recourse factoring, when the factor protects you when customers fail to pay. With non-recourse factoring the factor typically covers the risk by taking out credit insurance. The cost of the credit insurance will then be passed on to you at around 0.3–0.7 per cent of turnover, depending on the risk profile of your customers and the amount you factor. It is common now for most factors to offer you the facility of monitoring your account on the internet.

You will find a list of factors on the Asset Based Finance Association website (*www.abfa.org.uk*) or compare quotes from different factors on the Simply Business website (*www.simplybusiness.co.uk*).

Ask for extended credit terms with suppliers
Most businesses are looking to develop long-term relationships with their customers, which means there may be room to ask for extended credit from your suppliers. This usually means setting up an account, but a 30-day grace period before payment is due can make a huge difference to your cash flow.

Bathing Ape works hard to develop and maintain its brand identity to gain the trust of its customers. Likewise, you will need to develop and maintain a trust between yourself and your suppliers in order to obtain the most favourable payment terms

Negotiate a split delivery

With certain suppliers it may be worth seeing if it is possible to arrange a split delivery of goods. You may have a group of shops requiring delivery of their spring/summer stock in mid January whilst another group are more than happy to take delivery at the end of February. By negotiating a split delivery with your manufacturer you would first receive and pay for the goods needing to be sent out in January; 30 days later you would receive and pay for the remainder of the order.

Increasing borrowing, or putting more money into the business

You should consider this option only for dealing with short-term downturns in income or if you are looking to fund expansion of your business in line with your business plan. It should not form the foundation of your cash-flow strategy.

Top Tips for Improving Your Cash Flow

==

- ✘ *Issue invoices promptly and regularly chase outstanding payments.*
- ✘ *Consider exercising your right to charge penalty interest for late payment.*
- ✘ *Consider offering discounts for prompt payment (it's not uncommon for big department stores to tell you that they will take a percentage of the invoice for paying on time).*
- ✘ *Buy major items at the end rather than the start of a VAT period. This can greatly improve your cash flow – and may help plug a temporary cash-flow gap.*
- ✘ *Ask for a credit reference from other fashion labels that supply a new shop you are selling to, to see what kind of payers they are and therefore what terms you should offer.*
- ✘ *Make sure you deliver on time, to specification and with good quality to avoid any late or lost revenue.*
- ✘ *Target new customers efficiently to maximise income and minimise expenses.*
- ✘ *Make sure your suppliers are not overcharging and are delivering on time with good quality.*

==

Quite often the key to good cash flow for a small fashion business is to be as creative with your financial structures as you are with your design and marketing. Constantly monitor the situation in the same way as for new trends on the catwalk or high street. Look for opportunities to save money and negotiate where possible.

Cost of Goods Spreadsheet

Season:		Style Number:		
		Style Name:		

Piece Goods	Description	Cost Per Metre	Meterage Required	Cost
Fabric 1				
Fabric 2				
Fabric 3				
Lining				
Interfacing				
Other				
Allowance				
			Subtotal	

Trimmings	Description	Unit Cost	Number of Units	Cost
Buttons				
Zips				
Threads				
Labels				
Trims 1				
Trims 2				
			Subtotal	

Labour		Cost
Machinist		
Pattern cutting		
Grading		
Sewing		
	Subtotal	

Shipping		Cost
Bags/boxes		
Hangers		
Swing tickets		
Other		
	Subtotal	

Total Cost of Goods Sold	
Wholesale Mark-up	
Wholesale Price	
Retail Mark-up	
Recommended Retail Price	

Useful Websites

www.ecca-london.org – Enterprise Centre for the Creative Arts

www.fashioncapital.co.uk – Fashion Capital

www.fashion-enter.com – Fashion Enter

www.fashion-enterprise.com – Centre for Fashion Enterprise

www.businesslink.org.uk – Business Link

www.pbc.co.uk – Portobello Road Business Centre

www.craftcentral.org.uk – Craft Central

www.bbaa.org.uk – British Business Angels Association

www.hmrc.gov.uk – HM Revenue & Customs

www.5portlandplace.org.uk – No. 5 Portland Place (Centre of the UK Fashion Industry)

www.patent.gov.uk – Patent Office

Further Reading

Burns, Leslie Davis and Nancy O. Bryant, *The Business of Fashion: Designing, Manufacturing and Marketing*. New York: Fairchild, 1997

Fasanella, Kathleen, *The Entrepreneur's Guide To Sewn Product Manufacturing*. Fort Stanton, NM: Apparel Technical Services, 1998

Gehlhar, Mary, *The Fashion Designer Survival Guide: An Insider's Look at Starting and Running Your Own Fashion Business*. New York: Kaplan Business, 2005

Hines, Tony and Margaret Bruce, *Fashion Marketing: Contemporary Issues*. 2nd ed. Oxford: Butterworth-Heinemann, 2006

Jackson, Tim and David Shaw, eds., *The Fashion Handbook*. London and New York: Routledge, 2005

Jenkyn Jones, Sue, *Fashion Design*, 2nd ed. London: Laurence King Publishing, 2005

Johnson, Maurice J. and Evelyn C. Moore, *Apparel Product Development*. Upper Saddle River, NJ: Prentice Hall, 2001

Morris, Bethan, *Fashion Illustrator*. London: Laurence King Publishing, 2006

Okonkwo, Uche. *Luxury Fashion Branding: Trends, Tactics, Techniques*. Basingstoke: Palgrave Macmillan, 2007

Tungate, Mark, *Fashion Brands: Branding Style from Armani to Zara*. Sterling, VA: Kogan Page, 2005

Waddell, Gavin, *How Fashion Works: Couture, Ready-to-Wear and Mass Production*. Oxford: Wiley-Blackwell, 2004

Glossary

agent – person authorised to act on your behalf in selling your product.

bespoke – individually or custom made.

block – primary pattern used time and again allowing designers to modify key silhouettes.

boutique – small shopping outlet specialising in elite and fashionable items.

buyer – person responsible for purchasing your product from you in order to sell on to the consumer.

cash flow – measure of a company's financial health.

catwalk – where models parade the latest collections.

chain store – one of a number of retail stores under the same ownership and dealing in the same merchandise.

CMT – manufacturing terminology for Cut, Make, Trim.

comparative shopping – researching current products on the market offered by competitors.

copyright – exclusive legal right to reproduce, publish, sell, or distribute artistic work.

cottage industry – business or industry in which goods are produced primarily in the home of the producer.

cutting ticket – exact details for an actual order set for production otherwise know as the production run.

department store – large retail store offering a variety of merchandise and services.

discount store – store that sells merchandise at a discount from the manufacturer's suggested retail price.

distribution – supply and delivery of fashion goods to warehouses, shops and other outlets.

domain name – name that identifies a website.

eco fashion – fashion that is designed to be environmentally friendly.

editorial shoot – photographic spread that tells a story and creates an atmosphere.

entrepreneur – person that starts a new business venture.

exclusivity – one party grants another party sole rights with regard to a particular business function.

factor – third party provides the seller with cash by purchasing, or taking a lien against, the accounts receivable or inventories of the seller.

fashion cupboard – where fashion magazines organise/store garments called in for photographing.

fast fashion – fashion retailers buy their merchandise closer to the season, and hence respond to trends as they emerge.

fit model – model with standard proportions who tries on samples to get fit right.

franchise – right to market a product or provide a service as granted by a manufacturer or company.

full package manufacturing – manufacturer provides fully costed product including patterns, fabric, cut, make and all trims.

gross profit – profit before overhead (fixed operating expenses) has been deducted.

haute couture – exclusive clothes individually designed for private clients.

high end – expensive designs below haute couture level, often produced in limited numbers.

indirect cost – cost not directly attributable to the manufacturing of a product, also known as 'overhead'.

invoice – bill issued by the provider of products and/or services to a customer.

joint venture – entity formed between two or more parties to undertake economic activity together.

lead time – time taken for supplier to make goods available.

licensing – permission to use intellectual property rights, such as trademarks, patents, or technology, under defined conditions.

line sheet – selling tool showing sketches of product with pricing, colour options, sizes.

logo – name, symbol, or trademark designed for easy and definite recognition.

lookbook – marketing tool that shows photographs of collection.

made-to-measure – garment adjusted to customer's measurement.

margin – net sales minus the cost of goods and services sold.

mark-up – amount added to a cost price in calculating selling price.

mass-market fashion – ready-to-wear clothes produced in large quantities and standard sizes using cheaper materials.

minimums – smallest amount of goods a seller will allow a buyer to purchase.

moodboard – sketches, colours, images, ideas used as the starting point for designs and collections.

motif – sewn or printed decoration synonymous with a brand.

net profit – how much money a company has earned from doing business over the course of a year.

net sales – sales generated by a company after the deduction of returns, allowances for damaged or missing goods and any discounts allowed.

offer – product range put forward for purchase by the designer.

overhead – ongoing administrative expenses of a business, not attributed to any specific business activity, but still necessary for the business to function; also known as 'indirect cost'.

PDS – Pattern Design System, used to electronically cut and grade patterns.

pre-collection – delivered months ahead of designer's main catwalk ranges previewing new season's looks.

press book – folder for press cuttings.

press pack – collection of public relations material for distribution to the press.

press release – announcement of an event, performance, or other newsworthy item issued to the press.

prêt-à-porter – ready-to-wear clothing.

price architecture – framework in which you cost your products.

price point – standard price set by the seller for a product.

product portfolio – set of different products a fashion label produces.

pro forma – invoice presented for payment of goods prior to their dispatch.

ranges – styles and collections.

range plan – detailed structure of designer's collection prior to development of samples.

retail – sale of goods directly to the consumer.

ready-to-wear – clothing marketed in a finished condition, in standard clothing sizes.

RRP – Recommended Retail Price.

runway – another term for 'catwalk'.

samples – first versions of a design.

seasons – autumn/winter and spring/summer styles and collections.

sell-through rate – percentage of stock sold prior to mark-downs.

shelf life – time a product can be kept in store.

show card – card-mounted press clipping.

sourcing – researching, finding and obtaining materials, trimmings and finished garments.

specification drawing/spec – technical drawing showing all measurements of a product.

specification sheet – document including specification drawing, listing all the relevant components needed to make up a first sample.

speciality store – store selling only one type of merchandise.

split delivery – order delivered in more than one batch.

story board – summary of your collection's inspiration and theme.

supply chain – system of organising people, activities, information and resources to get product from manufacturer to customer.

swatch – small piece of fabric used to illustrate colour, print, design or detail before a piece is made or delivered.

swing ticket – tag put on products showing price, size and designer's logo/motif.

tear sheet – page cut or torn from a magazine, newspaper or journal.

toile – first made-up version of a garment in a cheap fabric.

turnover – total sales made in a given period of time.

unit price – cost or price of an item.

USP – Unique Selling Point.

wholesale – selling product to a retailer who sells on at a higher price.

working capital – cash available for day-to-day operations.

Index

Picture Credits

Ally Ward: 135; Belle & Bunty: 8, 53, 57, 65, 89, 106; Burton Retail Group: 11; Bread & Butter: 5, 6, 31, 37, 38, 60, 70, 73, 98, 118, 121, 122, 128, 147, 156; Caroline Charles: 76 (bottom), 96, 116–117; Daniel Garrett for the British Fashion Council: 12; David Hardy: 58, 102; Derek Henderson: 14, 56, 136–137; Ed Hardy: 36; Gil Carvalho: 28, 68–69, 111; Harrods: 87, 92, 133; Knomo: 27, 32, 42, 76 (top), 95, 151; PSC Photography: 41, 46, 146; London College of Fashion: 63; Magic: 123; Malcolm Crews: 138; Mizani: 150; Noir: 19, 20, 74, 83; Satoru Umetsu/ Nacasa & Partners: 79; Schumacher: 61, 91; Simon Walsh: 44–45; Three's Company (Creative Consultants) Ltd: 50, 107, 109, 141, 143, 154; TrendStop in conjunction with picture sourcing agent Fashionriot.com: 80. LKP would like to thank Geoff Fennell, Lewis Gill and Simon Walsh for their generous loans of bags and other designer paraphernalia photographed for the book.

Acknowledgements

My special thanks goes to:

My publisher Laurence King Publishing, in particular the commissioning editor Helen Evans for seeing the potential in the book, and Anne Townley and Melissa Danny for their experience, patience and perseverance in seeing me through the project.

Howard Harrison, Benoit Rescue and Alastair Hops at Knomo, Caroline Charles, Gil Carvalho, Karen Walker, Dorothee Schumacher, Anne Fontaine, Peter Ingwersen at Noir and Christian Audigier at Ed Hardy for all agreeing to be case studies and sharing their invaluable experiences. Also Kat and Oz Aalam, Simon Assirati, Suzanna Crabb, Malcolm Crews, Charlotte Kramer, Caroline Mackay, Rikard Osterlund, Nzinga Russell, Niki Turner, Ally Ward and Clare Watson for their contributions and authoritative views.

David Hardy, Malcolm Crews, Jaana Jätyri at Trendstop, Anna Millhouse and Rebecca Munro at London College of Fashion, Rupert Shreeve, British Fashion Council and London Fashion Week, and Marisa de Saracho at Magic International for their support with the visual content of the book.

My Belle & Bunty and Three's Company team including my business partners Alice Shreeve and Hannah Coniam for their constant support and inspiration, Lizzie Harper for all her help and patience no matter what the task, and Camille Boyd for her fantastic support in researching potential case studies.

Lastly I would like to give a big thank you to all my family and friends, and especially Alice, Mae and Yella to whom I dedicate this book.